Advance Praise for *Cutting Your Car Use*

Randall Ghent's *Cutting Your Car Use* is a lively,
useful, and humorous look at kicking our nasty national
habit: the unstoppable automobile. The facts are sound, and
the advice for the average drive-free-or-die car owner
is lively. Not just an agreeable read, but a fact-filled
and sound rationale of statistics and suggestions
that are both pragmatic and lively.

— JANE HOLTZ KAY, architecture/planning critic for
The Nation, and author of *Asphalt Nation*

Tired of traffic? Frustrated by rising fuel costs?
Concerned about climate change? "You can make a
difference," says *Cutting Your Car Use*. Ghent has packed
this great little back-pocket guide with essential tips telling
how we can all reap the benefits of driving less. This timely,
informative and easy-to-read handbook offers solutions.

— KATIE ALVORD, author of
*Divorce Your Car! Ending the Love Affair
with the Automobile*

Reducing dependence on the auto not only helps save the planet — it enriches your everyday life. This practical and inspiring guide offers all the details you need to make that break. You'll become more fit and less stressed, with extra money in your pocket and a satisfying feeling in your heart that you're making the world (and your town) a better place.

— JAY WALLJASPER, Executive Editor, *Ode* magazine & Senior Fellow, Project for Public Spaces

CUTTING your CAR USE

Cataloging in Publication Data:
A catalog record for this publication is available from the National Library of Canada.

Paperback ISBN 13: 978-0-86571-558-5
Paperback ISBN 10: 0-86571-558-0

Inquiries regarding requests to reprint all or part of *Cutting Your Car Use* should be addressed to New Society Publishers at the address below.

To discuss the bulk purchase of this book, please contact New Society Publishers, toll-free in North America, at 1 (800) 567-6772.
Outside of Canada, please call +1 (250) 247-9737.

To order directly from the publishers, please call toll-free (North America) 1 (800) 567-6772, or order online at www.newsociety.com

Any other inquiries can be directed by mail to:

New Society Publishers, P.O. Box 189, Gabriola Island, BC V0R 1X0, Canada 1 (800) 567-6772

New Society Publishers' mission is to publish books that contribute in fundamental ways to building an ecologically sustainable and just society, and to do so with the least possible impact on the environment, in a manner that models this vision. We are committed to doing this not just through education, but through action. We are acting on our commitment to the world's remaining ancient forests by phasing out our paper supply from ancient forests worldwide. This book is one step toward ending global deforestation and climate change. It is printed on acid-free paper that is **100% old growth forest-free** (100% post-consumer recycled), processed chlorine free, and printed with vegetable-based, low-VOC inks. For further information, or to browse our full list of books and purchase securely, visit our website at: www.newsociety.com

New Society Publishers   www.newsociety.com

save money, Be HeaLTHY, Be Green!

CUTTING your CAR USE

randall GHenT
WITH anna semLYen

cartoons by axel scheffler

NEW SOCIETY PUBLISHERS

Contents

- Introduction 1

1. Why Cut Your Car Use? .3
2. How Are You Using Your Car? 11
3. Looking at the Alternatives 23
4. Changing Your Travel habits 43
5. Making Better Use of Your Car 49
6. Living Without a Car 61
7. Carfree Places 69
8. Talking to Your Employer 73
9. Getting Active 77
10. The Rebound Effect 79

- Resources 81
- Appendix A: Greyhound and Amtrak Maps . . .105
- Appendix B: Metric Conversion 107
- Notes 109
- Acknowledgments 117
- About the Author 118

Introduction

Imagine a land where every child can walk or cycle to school in safety, where local businesses thrive, and a car is not essential to enjoy life. Picture how different your neighborhood would be with fewer moving cars. How much better would your life be if you were in a car less often? Cutting your car use will save you money, improve your health and improve everyone's quality of life.

Cutting Your Car Use gives practical advice on reducing traffic by changing personal habits. This book is for you if you are:

- Making transportation choices.
- Wanting to limit your driving, save money, be healthier and greener.
- Interested in starting a car-use reduction program at your school or workplace.
- Thinking of selling your car, carpooling or car sharing.

Many people think that there is too much car traffic. *You can make a difference.* There is a lot that you can do to tackle car dependency, and this book will show you how.

For specific and local information, consult the Resources at the back of this book. If you live in one of the 25 largest metropolitan areas in the US, or in one of the 10 largest in Canada, you'll find local transportation websites listed there.

Additional information can also often be found in the city or county pages in your local Yellow Pages directory.

All dollar figures in this book are in US dollars (with apologies to Canadian readers).

1

Why Cut Your Car Use?

Because our society has favored automobile-based development over the past century, cars have become useful in some situations and essential in others. Successfully cutting your car use in today's North American context involves forgoing unnecessary trips, choosing local businesses and facilities, getting exercise with walking and cycling, using car sharing and taking mass transit. Even if you could not manage without a car, or do not want a carfree lifestyle, there are many incentives for driving less, both financial and for a better quality of life.

US households spend nearly $1 in every $5 on driving.[1]

To Save Money

Are you driving to work, or working to drive? Do you know how much your car costs you? Use the table below to analyze your weekly car use and see what you could save by using some alternative means of transportation. What would you do with the money you save?

	From	To	Miles	Fuel $	Time	Alternative	Cost $	Time
Monday								
Tuesday								
Wednesday								
Thursday								
Friday								
Saturday								
Sunday								
TOTAL								

Estimate your household's total annual car costs and compare them with the US National Average[2] using the chart below:

	US National Average	Your Own Costs
Vehicle purchase costs (net outlay):	$3,664	_____
Finance charges on vehicle loans:	$371	_____
Gasoline and motor oil:	$1,333	_____
Vehicle insurance:	$905	_____
Maintenance and repair:	$619	_____
Rental, leases, licenses, other fees:	$436	_____
Total Annual Expenses:	$7,328	_____
Total Monthly Expenses:	$611	_____
Total Daily Expenses:	$20	_____

The AAA estimates that driving costs 56 cents per mile on average to operate a new domestic passenger car, or $8,410 per year. Cycling costs only about $220 per year.[3]

As the previous chart shows, the average American household (which has 1.8 drivers and 1.9 cars)[4] spends $20 a day on driving, every day of the year. That's about $10 a day per car. The AAA figure would put it at $23 a day per car. And if you thought gasoline is expensive now, a report called "The Real Price of Gasoline" finds that society pays an additional $4.60 to $14.14 per gallon in "external" costs not reflected in the price at the pump.[5]

Is your car worth the money it costs, and the time it takes to earn it? There are cheaper options:

- *Walk*: The cheapest and healthiest option of all.
- *Phone, text message, Internet and delivery*: These save time and reduce transportation costs.
- *Cycle*: Biking costs very little; folding bikes work well with elevators and mass transit.
- *Carpool*: Sharing rides means less driving; carpoolers usually split gasoline and toll costs as well.[6]
- *Mass transit*: A weekly or monthly pass can save you money.
- *Inter-city bus and train*: Often you can book online and in advance for special offers.

- *Car sharing and car rental*: When driving is the only convenient option, sharing or renting usually costs less than having a car on the road all the time.
- *Taxi*: As with sharing or renting, taxis are cheaper if you only rarely need your own car.

Owning and operating cars is the second largest household expense in the US. More is spent on the automobile than on food and clothing combined.[7]

With one less car, you could use taxis or car rental when necessary, and you could try out different car models to suit the purpose of the trip.

Bikesatwork.com/carfree offers a quick and easy online program that takes the amount of your total monthly car expenses (like in the previous chart) and calculates how much money you would have if you instead invested this amount in a retirement savings account, education savings account or home mortgage. The website also includes a "carfree census database" looking at where it's easiest to live without a car.

To Be Healthy
Air Quality
The air quality inside cars is typically much worse than outside. Cars on busy roadways drive through an invisible tunnel of concentrated pollutants, and carbon monoxide concentrations

may be more than 10 times higher than outside at the edge of the road, where walkers and cyclists tend to be.[8]

Atlanta, Georgia, initiated major citywide traffic reduction efforts during the 1996 Summer Olympic Games. Researchers there found that the rate of childhood asthma episodes requiring acute care fell dramatically during the games.[9]

—— *SUCCESS STORY* ——

If Ryan Lanyon and Dean Ross had owned a car, they wouldn't have been able to afford the house they bought in 2001 just outside downtown Ottawa, Ontario. Instead of driving, they commuted by foot, bicycle and transit to their jobs at the City of Ottawa and Bell Canada. Their house was built in 1907 and required considerable work. While doing house renovations and repairs can be a challenge without a car — and even more so without a bike trailer — Ryan often rode his bike back from the local Home Depot or Canadian Tire with his rear rack and wire baskets full of items such as a vacuum cleaner, a steam cleaner, a curtain rod, cans of paint and storage tubs. They had furniture and appliances delivered. In 2005 they moved to Toronto, where they continue to live carfree.

For every mile traveled on foot or by bicycle instead of by car, 2.6 grams of hydrocarbons, 20 grams of carbon monoxide, and 1.6 grams of nitrogen oxides are prevented from polluting the atmosphere.[10]

Exercise

Now for the good news! Walking is better than low salt diets for lowering blood pressure. It also increases bone mass and reduces fat.[11]

Cycling five miles, four times a week, can cut the risk of coronary heart disease by up to half.[12] In a trial, non-exercisers who began cycling around 19 miles a week rapidly improved their aerobic fitness by over 11%.[13] Cycling can also significantly reduce body fat.

Walking and cycling often give you the chance to use back roads and paths, reducing your exposure to traffic noise and fumes.

> **Regularly walking or cycling reduces risks of coronary heart disease by up to 50% and stroke by 66%.[14]**

To Be Green

Ground transportation is the fastest growing source of greenhouse gas emissions, which cause climate change. By driving less you can help fight global warming, improve air quality and enhance urban livability.

> **More than a quarter of all trips are one mile or less.[15] These trips could easily be made on foot, on skates or by bicycle.**

To Manage Time

Are you really saving time by driving? When you factor in the time you spend not just driving, but working to pay for your car expenses, cleaning and fixing your car, etc., if you're like the average American you put in 825 hours a year to go 12,000 miles. You're driving 31.5 mph on average, but your "real speed" (12,000 miles divided by 825 hours), is only 14.5 miles per hour — the pace of a brisk bicycle ride.[16]

That's a conservative figure. Your "real speed" could be as low as walking pace if you have an expensive car, drive mostly on urban (slower) roads, and/or don't drive a great deal. Why not save the hassle of car ownership, when you're not really going any faster than a pedestrian? And if you factor in the 30 minutes per day that you should be exercising, assuming you drive at least 30 minutes per day, that would add on 183 hours in lost exercise time every year caused by driving (rather than walking or cycling, which provide exercise). That would pull our original "real speed" figure down to 12 mph.

- Could you cut your "chauffeur" duty by giving your children bus passes or by arranging a carpool?
- Could you telecommute, or work while you commute on mass transit?

The most important thing is to *make a start*. Begin by experimenting with traveling less or using alternatives.

———— *SUCCESS STORY* ————

Megan Wilson of Cleveland, Ohio, grew up borrowing her parents' cars, until she saved up the money to buy Grandma's '96 Oldsmobile Eighty-Eight. Six months later, while the luxury "living room on wheels" was parked overnight, it was hit by a drunk driver. Megan considered this a blessing — and as a sign from her grandmother, who had died only two weeks before — that it was time to live the lifestyle she wished for. She took the insurance settlement and went on a South American vacation. When she came back, she fixed up her bicycle, bought a helmet, and hasn't looked back. Now she cycles everywhere, and sometimes takes advantage of the bike racks attached to the front of the city buses. Her co-workers call her "Super-woman" for her quick changes in the office restroom, from sweats into suit and heels in two minutes or less. She's lost a lot of weight, and for the first time in her life, she feels really, honestly strong. She now organizes a support group called Carfree in Cleveland.

2

How Are You Using Your Car?

If you want to drive less, start by analyzing how and why you travel. "Location, location, location" is a catchphrase in the property market, and it applies to all activities when trying to cut your car use. Aim to reduce your need to travel.

Commuting
You can change your travel behavior in small ways and reap the benefits. You don't necessarily have to make major lifestyle changes.

- If possible, choose work by its proximity to your home, or choose to live near good public transportation links.
- Try walking, cycling, mass transit and/or carpooling. Trip planner websites for many US and Canadian cities are listed in the Resources.
- If you are a shift worker, ask to work shifts with people you could carpool with.
- Request flexible working hours. Then being slightly late or early is no problem and you can fit your hours around timetables. The US Department of Labor offers several documents about flexible hours. (Dol.gov/dol/topic/workhours/flexibleschedules.htm)

- Ask for compressed working (when you can take a day off if hours are worked in advance). There was a 16% cut in sick leave after its introduction in Irvine, California.[1] Working nine rather than ten days every two weeks means a 10% reduction in commuting.
- If possible, work at home. This saves your employer money by saving on office space and other office resources.

- Consider part-time work. Being carfree may save a day's net wages weekly.
- Talk to managers about Commuter Choice options. See Chapter 8 (Talking with Your Employer) for details and contacts.

In the US, 15% of car trips are for traveling to and from work.[2]

On-the-Job Trips

You generally have less choice over your business travel than over how you get to and from work, so when applying for a job, ask about:

- Travel policy — is there a Commuter Choice program?
- Details of lump sum and/or mileage allowances for driving/cycling/walking.
- Refunds for delivery services, public transport, taxi fares or discount travel passes.
- Availability of carpool vehicles, folding bicycles, or a car sharing system (one that includes priority parking and guarantees a taxi home if car sharing fails).

If you use a car in the course of your work, try to reduce mileage when planning your trips.

For urban trips, cycling beats a car in peak hours and is quicker than a bus for trips up to 8 miles.[3]

Trips to School

The trip to school is usually the first trip of the day. It affects children's health and future transportation habits. The school run represents 20–25% of morning traffic; 50% of children hit by cars near schools are hit by parents of other students.[4]

Travel Awareness

- Choose your nearest school and consider relocating or working nearer if necessary.
- Teach children road and personal safety.
- Choose a quiet route if possible and walk or cycle together.
- Familiarize your children with local public transportation, timetables and independent travel.
- Make children aware of the locations of hazards on their normal route(s), such as busy streets that they will need to cross.
- Hang up local walking, cycling and public transportation maps at home.

Working with Your Child's School

Schools can take many initiatives to cut school traffic and make it safer for walkers and cyclists:

- Distribute "safe routes to school" maps.
- Organize a "walking or cycling school bus," in which an adult collects children along a prearranged route. In Chicago, 175 schools participate in the Walking School Bus program, and nearly 90% of the city's 422,000 public school children walk to school.[5]
- Run/endorse a carpool program.
- Give out reflective clothing.
- Request lower speed limits on approach roads (20 mph/30 kph).

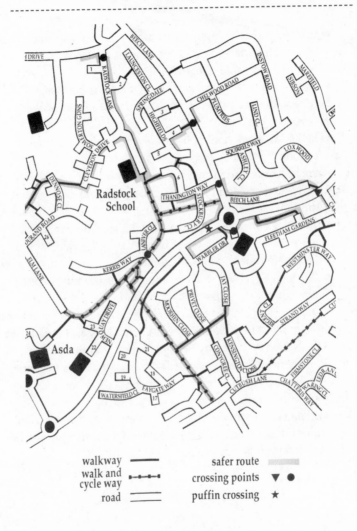

An example of a safe route to school map, produced by Living Streets, UK.

- Create safe crossings, with traffic calming measures and/or crossing guards. Some schools designate drop-off points to avoid congestion.
- Have carfree school entrances — create a pedestrian-only gathering place or public square in front of the school.
- Hold cars back until pedestrians and cyclists have left school.
- Have secure and visible cycle shelters.
- Have lockers or storage for books, cycling gear and outdoor clothing.
- To reduce the weight of bags/backpacks, do a home-work review to see if fewer books can be carried.
- Use "safe routes" as a class topic.
- Put up a school travel notice board with maps, timetables and carpooling information.

A free toolkit titled "Safe Routes to School" is available from the US National Highway Traffic Safety Administration. It provides educators and others with materials to promote walking and biking to school. It includes sections on mapping the routes to school, activities and outreach, and classroom lessons, press releases, posters and more. See Walktoschool-usa.org/srts-start/. In Canada, a wealth of information can be found at Saferoutestoschool.ca.

> ─── *SUCCESS STORY* ───
>
> Nine-year-old Blake Tiede lives with his family and his lop-eared rabbit Snowball in the quiet, upscale town of Dunwoody, just outside of Atlanta, Georgia. He's an outgoing and active "gentle giant," growing his own garden, playing lots of sports, raising money to fight juvenile diabetes, winning blue ribbons for "best youth float" in the local parade, and leading his Cub Scout pack in popcorn sales. Blake walks to school, to Dunwoody Village, and to the swim club, where he can often be found playing Sharks and Minnows. Walking "wakes me up early in the morning" and is a good time to see friends on the way to school. He likes walking home as a way to "unwind" from the day, and to invite a friend over to play. However, until 2005, Blake and his schoolmates had no sidewalk on which to walk the half-mile to Austin Elementary, through the neighborhood of traditional Georgian homes. But Blake and the Dunwoody Homeowner Association lobbied the county commissioners, and after two years of work, there's now a sidewalk where none existed. The new sidewalk is safer for everybody, and as a result, more kids walk and bike to school.

Shopping Trips

In the US, 45% of all trips are for shopping and errands.[6] Instead of driving, you could explore some of the following options:

- Walk or cycle to local stores and farmers' markets.

- When cycling, use a bike trailer, panniers or basket to carry loads.
- Take a taxi to buy in bulk, or share a car or taxi with neighbors.
- Use mail-order businesses and Internet shopping.
- Consider growing and cooking more of your food yourself, or joining a Community-Supported Agriculture program to buy local produce.

*One basket of imported produce could release as much CO_2 into the atmosphere as an average four-bedroom household does through cooking meals for eight months.
So buying more locally makes the most sense.*[7]

—— *SUCCESS STORY* ——

Lisa Brown of Orlando, Florida, is a single mother of two teenage boys with developmental disabilities. They use a combination of walking, biking and public buses. Lisa always wanted to live a more environmentally friendly lifestyle and hated driving her gas-guzzling 1995 Ford Aerostar. She had been planning to replace the van with a hybrid, but when the van died, she decided not to replace it. Instead she bought monthly bus passes for the family. Whereas before Lisa had been forever lost and frustrated when driving around Orlando, now the family takes adventures, enjoying the exercise and the freedom of not having to find a parking space. They've discovered a park and a lake within walking distance of the central library, where they go to see the black swans, fish and turtles. She's found that the bus schedules are sometimes inconvenient, and that carrying some items aboard can be difficult, so she's alleviated the problem by cycling instead, using bicycle baskets, and she plans to buy a bike trailer to carry more cargo. Although Florida is hot and rainy, Lisa is still not inclined to buy a car in the near future. She's even working on getting her sons in shape so they can start taking long-distance bike tours.

- Buy as locally as possible. Minimize your use of products (especially heavy items) shipped from far away. For example, if you live in California, try to resist that imported wine. This decreases the amount of driving and shipping required to bring products to you.

Portland State University professor Jan Semenza grew up in Switzerland, where the urban landscape is much more pedestrian friendly than in America. When he moved to Portland, Oregon, in 1999 he did not like how the grid layout of the city favored traffic over public life. Jan started hosting Sunday brunches in his home to encourage community building. Out of this formed a neighborhood group, and they quickly developed a plan to take back the streets from crime, traffic, drug use and litter. With approval from the city and help from The City Repair Project, they converted the intersection of Southeast 33rd Avenue and Yamhill Street into "Sunnyside Piazza." Now a painting of a giant sunflower fills the street surface of the entire intersection, and several interactive art features adorn the neighboring yards. Jan and his neighbors have gone on create street murals, art structures, hanging gardens and information kiosks — all part of a human-scale urban landscape that encourages walking. Now that his neighborhood has become a destination for pedestrians and bikers and great place to be, Jan rarely uses his car.

Home Deliveries

- Many supermarkets, restaurants and some local stores offer delivery services, either through online ordering, telephone or fax.
- Use home deliveries for furniture, large appliances and other heavy, bulky goods.

- Wholesale distributors of non-perishable foods will often do home deliveries if you make a bulk order (perhaps combined with friends), saving you lots of money.
- Find other companies that offer home delivery.

Social Trips

Try to plan your social activities with minimal use of a car.

- When sending out invitations, include a map and travel information with auto-alternatives.
- Walking and cycling provide more opportunities to meet and talk to people than driving.
- Make local contacts by visiting local rather than distant destinations.

Recreational Trips

Trips to the countryside are a reason given for car ownership, but many towns, villages, tourist attractions and recreational destinations can be reached by public transportation. Find locally based hobbies and leisure pursuits — explore from your door. Get to know your nearby parks and open space.

3

Looking at the Alternatives

Walking

Walking is an excellent alternative to driving, with many benefits, including:

- It's inexpensive.
- It's healthy — even 20 minutes a day makes a big difference.
- Walking reduces the chance of getting cancer, heart disease, stroke, diabetes and other diseases. Pedestrians live longer and get mental health and spiritual benefits.[1]
- Getting out on foot gives you the opportunity to meet people en route.
- Walking allows you to become more familiar with your surroundings.

More than one-quarter of all trips are one mile or less. At least 123 million car trips made each day in the US are short enough to have been made on foot.[2]

No matter how much you drive, every trip begins and ends on foot. For short trips and sometimes for longer journeys, walking is the way to go.

- A list of local walking organizations can be found at Americawalks.org.
- The US Surgeon General recommends getting 30 minutes of exercise most days of the week; walking more often can help you attain that goal.
- Just how walkable is your community? Use the easy-to-use checklist at Walkableamerica.org to help you decide.

Carpooling

75.7% of US workers and 73.8% of Canadian workers commute alone via car, truck or van.[3]

Lots of people share cars regularly, with friends and family, without thinking about it. But there are times when drivers have empty seats because they don't know anyone who needs a lift. Organized carpooling is one solution. In fact, 12.2% of American workers already carpool.[4]

Carpooling benefits you, the community and the environment. It reduces travel costs; lessens congestion, pollution and parking problems; can eliminate the need for a private car; and is a solution to public transportation problems. It is also a way to meet like-minded people.

- Register with Carpoolconnect.com (US), and search its database of commuters in your area going where you're going. In Canada, try Commuter Connections (Carpool.ca), Canada's leading rideshare program. There are many other websites too, including local ones, as well as non-Internet-based carpools. You'll be matched with someone to share the trip and its costs.
- Use "Park & Ride" sites. This is when people travel independently to a meeting point and then take a public bus or minivan to a common destination, such as downtown from a parking lot next to a freeway.
- The cost of fuel is rising, with no real reversal likely. With carpoolers to share the cost, carrying one passenger can cut the fuel cost in half; two passengers could entirely cover the costs.

Before sharing, keep in mind some basic safety guidelines:

- Avoid exchanging home addresses with your traveling companions before you meet them.
- Arrange to meet in a public place.
- Arrange to meet near mass transit, so you have an alternative if the ride falls through.
- Tell a friend or family member when and where you are traveling, and with whom.

- The first time you lift share with a stranger, satisfy yourself as to his or her identity. You could ask for identification, such as a passport, student card or driver's license.

SUCCESS STORY

Aaron von Flatern was the son of a Texas oilfield worker, then became a Texas oilfield worker, then a college graduate, and then, somehow, an insurance adjuster. He settled in Houston, a city somewhat proud of its 50-plus miles of strip-mall-coated highways. Aaron kept adjusting car crash claims and as his skill progressed, so did the seriousness of the crashes. He remembers a photo of a dead man dangling by his seat belt from the open door of what no longer looked like his pick-up truck. Aaron sometimes dreamt about car accidents, sometimes would have anxiety attacks in traffic. It never really occurred to him to walk to beat stress. But in 2004, at age 27, he started walking and taking the bus to work — to impress a girl who liked environmental types. However, what kept him walking, what made him eventually abandon his car for days at a time, far exceeded his desire to impress the girl. Walking gave Aaron a feeling of adventure and indescribable childish happiness ... of community, innocence, pride and hope. He's become an active pedestrian advocate and has never felt more inspired. In fact, he is now an environmental type — a real one.

Taxis

Taxis are convenient, available 24 hours, and save you from searching for a parking place or worrying about directions. If you plan to drink, they're also safer.

- Taxis cost less than rental cars for the first 30 miles or so.
- To cut costs even further, share a taxi with others going to the same destination.

For the cost of owning and operating an average new domestic car, you could spend $23 a day on taxis.[5]

Cycling

Modern gears and a lightweight frame and components make for an easier ride. If you are unsure what to buy you could rent a bike for a while to help you decide. It's important that your bicycle be comfortable and well-fitting; any bike shop will help you choose a properly fitting bike.

- Cyclists enjoy more reliable travel times than car users.
- 40% of Americans say they would commute by bike if safe facilities were available.[6]
- Cycling is healthy, clean, quiet and poses little risk to others.
- Cycling is the most energy efficient and least polluting of any mode of transportation. Yet it is the most neglected means of travel in the US: less than 1% of all

----

trips in American cities are by bicycle. By contrast, cycling accounts for 28% of urban trips in the Netherlands, 20% in Denmark, 12% in Germany and 10% in Switzerland.[7]

- Folding bikes can fit on a train, subway, bus, coach, taxi or ferry and give you more flexibility than using bike racks on a car. See the Resources section for more information on finding folding bikes.

The Better World Club (BWC) offers the first and, at this time of writing, the only bicycle roadside assistance service in the US. It costs $40 per year (2006), with coverage up to 30 miles and two service calls per year. Adding more people to the same membership costs $15 each, to a maximum of four people. BWC members also receive a free membership to the League of American Bicyclists, a $30 value which includes a subscription to *Bicycling* magazine and a number of other benefits. Alternatively, bicycle coverage can be added to any of the club's auto coverage programs for $15.

An estimated 131 million Americans regularly bicycle or walk for sport, exercise, recreation or pure enjoyment.[8]

Safety

- A bike helmet is recommended, and in some areas is required by law. Protection will vary according to fitting, speed and other factors. See Cyclehelmets.org for information, or ask at your local bike store. Gloves are also a good idea.

- Front and rear bicycle lights are vital at night, and again, may be required by law in some areas. Some LED lights last for many hours even with rechargeable batteries (e.g., nickel-metal-hydrides). Dynamo-powered lights are another alternative.
- Make sure you are seen. Use maximum-visibility pedals, put reflectors on your bike and wear reflective clothing if possible. Look for puncture-resistant tires with a reflective strip.
- If you are new to a bike, you might want to avoid major roads, difficult intersections or left turns. Read the online guide "How to Not Get Hit by Cars," at Bicycle safe.com.
- Consider insurance for personal accident, injury and theft, or check your existing policies to see if bicycle coverage is included or can be added.

Maintenance

- Keep tires inflated to the pressure shown on the tire.
- Check that you can rock the front of the bike by the handlebars with the front brake on without movement of the headset (the bolt your handlebar stem slots into).
- Check that brakes and gears are working efficiently with cables that are not frayed.
- Clean and lubricate the chain with synthetic dry lube such as Tri-Flow, Pedro's or Finish Line.
- Check chain tension. It should be firm, not sloppy.
- Correct saddle height is when, with your heel on the lower pedal, your leg is almost straight.

―――――― *SUCCESS STORY* ――――――

Rich Points moved to Boulder, Colorado, in 1998 to go to grad school and began biking all the time. He sold his truck a year later, since Boulder is one of the best places in the US to bicycle. He's been carfree ever since. "I hope to never own an automobile again," he says. The infrastructure in Boulder is great, with over 300 miles of bike lanes, multi-use paths and open space trails. In 2004 the League of American Bicyclists awarded Boulder a gold medal for bicycle friendliness. Rich is active with the Boulder Bicycle Commuters, a group that works with the city council, local businesses and citizens to further improve conditions for cycling. "I'm no lone soul here," Rich says. "There are many carfree folks, some of whom have been carfree for 40+ years."

Secure your Bike

- Buy a good lock — D-lock models are usually best, but are not all created equal. Choose a medium-quality ($20+) or high-quality ($40+) model, based on what you can afford. Kryptonite (see Kryptonitelock. com) is the brand to look for, and is available at most bike shops.
- If you live in a theft-prone area, you have three choices: buy an expensive lock, ride a cheap bike (the low-stress option), or always keep your bike with you or secured indoors.

- A folding bike kept with you is unlikely to be stolen.
- If you go the expensive lock route, Kryptonite offers the "New York Fahgettaboudit" lock ($100+), which should deter or confound any potential thief. The company is so confident about this lock that it offers $3,500 in anti-theft protection in the US and Canada. The similar but slightly less tough "New York Chain" and the D-lock equivalent "New York 3000 Lock" sell for $65–80 and offer $3,000 in anti-theft protection.
- You can find much cheaper D-lock models that still offer $1,000+ in anti-theft protection.
- Buy an inconspicuous, inexpensive bicycle. Larger BMX and mountain bikes are stolen twice as often as other types.[5] Unusual, women's or visually unattractive models face less risk.
- When you leave your bike, lock it to an immovable object. Remember to secure any quick release parts, or get them replaced with fixed versions.
- Note your bicycle's make, color and frame number.

- Get your bicycle registered, by going to your local police station.

Only 8% of thefts involve cracking a D or U lock.
Crime prevention officers say that if all cyclists used
high quality D-Locks, theft could fall by 5–90%.[9]

Electric Bicycles

You can largely overcome hills and headwinds with a power-assisted bicycle. These are available from several companies listed in the Resources. Also available are power kits to be used with normal bicycles.

Riding an electric bike doesn't require a license, registration or insurance. See Electric-bikes.com for details.

- A friction-drive kit is an easily installed, low-cost unit, but is affected by rain.
- A purpose-built hub drive is most efficient, quiet and reliable.
- Friction drives and cheap hubs have a finite life, while crank motors, chain-drive motors and quality hubs should last a lifetime.
- Chain-driven rear wheel or pedal crankshaft bikes are purpose-built and efficient.
- Folding models and tricycles are also available.
- An electric bicycle will go an average of 15 powered miles at 14 mph before recharging.

Batteries

For battery-driven power bicycles, lead-acid gel-cell batteries are cheap, easy to maintain and reliable but output gradually diminishes if not serviced. Nickel-cadmium batteries (nicads) hold 25% more energy by weight, but cost more and are a disposal hazard (you could ask the manufacturer to take them back). The newer nickel-metal-hydride batteries are slightly better environmentally.

Local Public Transportation

- Public transportation is often cheaper than driving, even for two adults. A professional driver is at least twice as safe as driving yourself, and there is no parking hassle.
- In an increasing number of places, public buses have bike racks installed on the front. Ask your local bus service to offer this.
- The American Public Transportation Association website (Apta.com) has links to every local, regional and inter-city public transportation service in North America.
- The range of fares — including discounts for children, students and seniors — is usually listed in a printed timetable brochure available inside the bus.
- It's often possible to print out timetables from the Internet.
- For transportation for the physically disabled, check your local *Yellow Pages* or contact your county public services department.
- In some larger cities, of course, you'll find subway systems.

An increasing number of cities offer light rail, the modern equivalent of the old trolley cars. Light rail has dedicated tracks and therefore doesn't get slowed down by car traffic. In addition to the city's famous cable cars and its BART, MUNI and bus networks, San Francisco has brought back the old-style trolleys along Market Street. These are trolley cars left over from the systems scrapped across America in the 1930s–1950s after having been bought out by General Motors, Firestone Tire and other automobile interests.[10]

For every dollar invested in public transit, three dollars in business revenue are generated. Further, transit investment in the US over the past 30 years has alleviated the need for spending $220 billion on the building of parking spaces and additional lane miles of freeway and arterial roads.[11]

Trains

Trains are generally more expensive than buses, and routes are much more limited. But it's a comfortable, enjoyable way to

travel. Despite high-profile disasters, rail travel is statistically much safer than driving,[12] and can be faster than a car over long distances or in congested areas. Amtrak provides most of the train service in the US, while VIA Rail and some Amtrak routes serve Canada (see Appendix A).

The Resources section provides detailed information (2006) about discounts and packages for Amtrak, as well as listing some lesser-known train services.

In Canada, VIA Rail offers regular passenger discounts for advanced ticket sales, students, seniors, groups and families. For more information, see the Resources section or Viarail.ca.

SUCCESS STORY

Emily Brewer and her husband live near Chapel Hill, North Carolina, where the buses are free, all the time, every day. They own two cars, but chose their apartment because it's near a convenient bus route to the University of North Carolina, where Emily teaches and studies — and where parking is extremely limited. While she had never used public transit regularly before moving to town, Emily now only drives once or twice a month at most. She even takes the bus when going off-campus, even though driving is faster and parking is usually available. Why? Several years ago she developed asthma and allergies, and has become keenly aware of air pollution. "I can just 'feel' it more than others," she says. "If I have to drive to get somewhere, I often won't go, in part because it would be contributing to an already tainted air supply." There's a social benefit, too. On the bus, Emily hears political commentary, mothers chatting with their little ones, local youth recounting the day's events, and librarians discussing the comparative merits of working at the reference desk or in Interlibrary Loan. "I really feel like I know my community better for riding the bus," she says.

Inter-City Buses

Buses are a safe way to travel, and cost less than train tickets, but the trip can take longer and be less comfortable. Greyhound serves over 3,300 destinations throughout the US, Canada and Mexico. The Trailways franchise and other companies offer regional service. Green Tortoise is a more alternative company that leads "adventure travel" throughout the US and Mexico, going slowly but offering nice food and stops at hot springs and such along the way. Jefferson Lines runs daily inter-city bus service in 11 states throughout the US and Canada, extending from Dallas to Winnipeg. See the Resources section for information about other bus companies.

Car Rental

If you need a car for longer trips, considering renting a car for all or part of the journey.

- Look for discounts from combining car rental with hotel stays or travel tickets.
- Some rental car companies have membership or loyalty discounts (10% plus), fast-track service, online booking discounts, hotel discounts or programs that give you frequent-flyer mileage with a participating airline.

In a year, you can get 51 single days of car rental annually for less than the fixed costs of owning a small used car.[13]

Car Sharing Clubs

Car sharing clubs offer access to a range of vehicles without the hassle and expense of ownership. Cars are parked in designated places around town and can be booked for as little as an hour by Internet or phone. The overall effect is that each shared car replaces 7–10 private cars, resulting in less need for parking spaces. People who join a car sharing club tend to reduce their driving by up to 50%.[14]

Drivers typically pay an annual membership fee, plus an hourly, daily or monthly rate for car use. Hourly rates tend to be $8–10 and daily rates about $60 — usually including gas, insurance and unlimited miles. Discounted plans for regular users are available. If you drive less than 8,000 miles (13,000 km) per year, car sharing probably makes more sense than car ownership. Check the various plans available to find out.

Other member benefits might include:

- A variety of vehicles available to suit each particular trip.
- Inclusion of tax, parking and/or maintenance costs.
- Full breakdown coverage, and 24/7 roadside assistance.
- Cars are normally less than three years old.
- Discounts with participating businesses.

See the Resources section for a listing of car sharing clubs. Car sharing is growing in popularity, and clubs are popping up in an increasing number of cities. See Carsharing.net for a listing of car sharing clubs across North America and abroad. Zipcar and Flexcar are for-profit car sharing clubs that operate in multiple cities. Both received major new financial backing in 2005, so you can expect to hear more from them soon. Zipcar.com offers a travel costs spreadsheet to calculate the savings to be made by being a car club member. For more information about car sharing clubs, visit Carsharing.net.

—————— *SUCCESS STORY* ——————

When Jeanne Wood moved back to Edmonton, Alberta in 1996 (from London, England, and Toronto, Ontario), she had a new appreciation of Edmonton's lower cost of living and the fact that she could afford to live centrally and either walk or take the bus to wherever she needed to go. She rented an apartment in Edmonton's historic Old Strathcona district, an easy ten-minute bus ride downtown, where she works. Because Jeanne lives and works in such a central location, she has her choice of buses and routes. This is especially useful in Edmonton's very cold winter months, because it limits the time spent outdoors. In 2001, Jeanne joined the local car sharing co-op, to have access to a vehicle for occasional errands. For Jeanne, car sharing is the perfect solution. Environmental concerns aside, car ownership doesn't make economic sense for her: A monthly bus pass costs less than a parking space downtown, and that doesn't even begin to take into account the cost of buying or leasing a car, insurance and fuel. Jeanne is also very committed to public transportation, and feels it's important to support Edmonton's transit system.

Sharing Car Ownership

By sharing a car, you can save 50% or more on all your fixed ownership and operating costs. You could set up a car club with friends, neighbors or colleagues, either with a car already owned or by purchasing together. You will need to consider:

- Responsibility for servicing, maintenance and insurance.
- How you will pay for it; for example, splitting fixed costs according to time used, or running costs by mileage.
- How the car will be booked; where it will be parked.
- How to prioritize usage; for instance, will one person have priority at particular times, certain days of the week, or will it be first come, first served? Could you use car rental as a back up?
- A booking system; for example, a diary or wall chart/stickers.
- A system for recording use, such as recording miles in a logbook.
- Gasoline use — sharers usually pay for their own gasoline, so you could agree to fill the tank before swapping over, or note gas costs and miles driven.
- Tax and other issues.
- How the sharing arrangement will end if someone decides they want to leave.

Mopeds, Scooters and Motorcycles

Powered two-wheelers are cheaper to run, easier to park, can be quicker than cars, and take up less road space. However, you may have safety concerns. Also a typical gas-powered scooter is very noisy and can emit 5–10 times the air pollution as the average automobile.[15] Ask your local Department of Motor Vehicles about the licensing requirements for driving a scooter or motorbike.

Even though more stringent emissions and noise standards for gas-powered scooters are on the way, an electric scooter is a far better option. The Vectrix Electric Maxi-Scooter, available from 2006, is billed as "the world's first, truly practical, zero-emission alternative to traditional gasoline-powered motorcycles and scooters." It offers the benefits of gasoline power but without the noise, pollution, expensive maintenance, frequent oil changes, and regular trips to the gas station. With a top speed of 62 mph and a battery range of 68 miles (at 25 mph), the Vectrix scooter is the first electric scooter capable of outperforming its gasoline-powered equivalents, according to the company. Vectrix also offers a fuel-cell hybrid version. For more information, see Vectrixusa.com.

Other Alternatives

There are many occasions when a bicycle won't serve the purpose, yet a car would be overkill — like carving a turkey with a chainsaw. Sometimes the only good reason to use a car is because they are omnipresent — people either own them or can buy one almost anywhere. However, if you do a bit of searching, you can find an amazing variety of well-tested, high-performance vehicles that run on human power, electricity or both. Many of the companies that produce these are in the Resources section.

In-line skates, for example, have a feel similar to ice skating. It's quicker than walking, greener and healthier than car use, and does not take much practice. Choose recreational blades, which are faster and more durable (they're longer than "aggressives" and have a heel brake). Good blades start around $65. For information on good deals on all kinds of skates and skating equipment, see Skates.com.

Skateboarding or using a push scooter is two to three times faster than walking. Boards can be very light, and fit easily under your arm or can be attached to a bag when not in use. Utility skaters need good bearings with big, soft wheels, and should wear protective pads.

—— *SUCCESS STORY* ——

Chuck Boyce is a database administrator for a large health insurance company in Philadelphia. In 2002, a friend introduced Chuck to the idea of car sharing. Being a self-described "major geek," the whole sign up online thing really stuck in Chuck's memory. Time went by and he got increasingly annoyed at the hassle of maintaining a car that he only drove one day a week — to see his parents out in the suburbs. He finally decided to try car sharing. Instead of justifying to himself why it was cost effective to drive an old beater around town, he now "really digs cruising about in a happening new hybrid." One day Chuck mentioned the car-sharing club to the manager of his apartment building, who loved the idea, so now there's a free parking spot right outside the building — in contrast to the $30,000 parking spaces for sale in the new garage across the street. Chuck says "car sharing totally rocks!"

4

Changing Your Travel Habits

The Psychology of Changing

Morning decisions are crucial! Habit and your first choice of transportation influence how you get around for the rest of the day. Think about your first trip of each day and then try changing it for the better. If you are in a hurry, have a lot to carry, or are traveling at night, you may not feel like walking or cycling, so:

- Plan the alternatives for regular first journeys. What type of transportation, route, time, with whom, etc.
- Allow time for walking or cycling. Don't aim to fit in too much, particularly on your first trip.
- Get everything you need for your alternative travel ready the night before.
- Try to travel in daylight.
- Minimize what you carry, particularly on the first trip. Use lockers, delivery or good load-carrying aids.

Set Yourself Targets

Following are some examples of goals you can set:

1. My car use is _____ miles a year. I aim to cut it by ____ % in 6 months, by ____ % in a year to under _____ miles per year.

2. I am usually in a car ____ days a week. I aim to use a car on only ____ days a week by _____ (date).

3. My car's engine capacity is _____ cc. I aim to get a smaller car with a _____ cc engine and better fuel efficiency by _____ (date).

4. My household has ____ car(s). I aim reduce it to ____ car(s) by _____ (date).

Check your progress at six months, and again at twelve. Reward yourself when you reach one of your targets. Then set a new goal.

Some people deliberately make choosing car travel harder, for example:

- Parking the car at a good walking distance from the door.
- Sharing a car or lending it to (insured) drivers to limit availability/temptation.
- Hanging up car keys rather than keeping them in your bag or pocket.
- Deciding not to drive at all on certain days of the week.
- Saving up all car-related errands for an allotted day of the week.

Stop and Think

Ask yourself: "Is the car really necessary?" A car-dependent person will think no further about how to travel — only driving comes to mind. Habits are created by practice, and can be changed! Ask yourself:

- Why am I traveling?
- Do I really need to travel? If so, how far? Is there a nearer alternative?
- Can I link the trip with another purpose?
- How shall I travel?
- Is there public transportation? Can I rearrange to fit timetables?
- Can I share the ride or vehicle costs?

Localize

> *One quarter of all trips are one mile or less,*
> *but three quarters of these short trips are made by car.*
> *The average American motorist drives 29 miles a day*
> *and spends 55 minutes a day behind the wheel.[1]*

Using local goods and services is convenient, saves time, money and the earth's resources, and supports your local economy rather than big business. Make some time for yourself by:

- Using letters, phone, fax, e-mail or delivery instead of traveling.
- Combining trips by traveling for two or more purposes.

Travel Carefree and Carfree

And finally, in what is hopefully a sign of things to come elsewhere, there are now at least three websites providing a range of travel information for visiting specific places without a car:

- Santabarbaracarfree.org is an initiative led by the Santa Barbara County Air Pollution Control District (CA). "The idea is not to take all cars off the streets, but to help people take advantage of carfree alternatives."

The initiative involves many other partners, including Amtrak, which offers a discount with the headline "Travel Car-Free to Santa Barbara and Save!"

- Smartguide.org promotes carfree travel to Cape Cod, Martha's Vineyard and Nantucket (MA).
- Exploreacadia.com offers a "Car-Free Travel Guide" for Acadia National Park in Maine.

SUCCESS STORY

Barbara Scott is a professional event planner who loves her work and nearly everything about her native Seattle. "People pay me to plan parties, for goodness' sake!" The one thing she doesn't love is the city's horrific traffic and the stress that it creates in her. To improve her health, she decided to try living carfree. She moved to Capitol Hill to a quiet street with plenty of restaurants, grocery stores and other businesses within a short walk. Both her bank and the post office are less than two blocks from her home. Using cars has always made Barbara feel a bit guilty, and she's always happier when she doesn't have to drive. She normally walks, cycles or takes the bus. On the occasions when she does still need a car, she uses car sharing or, more rarely, rents a car over a weekend after bunching up a number of errands and appointments to maximize her use of the vehicle. Barbara has chosen to go against the tide of car ownership and, for her, it is a much healthier choice.

5

Making Better Use of Your Car

If you decide to keep your car, what changes can you make to use it less? Can you plan some days without meetings, or carpool even a few days a week?

Plan Your Trips

In order to analyze your car use, record a personal diary of all car trips for a week. Then see if you can reduce your need to travel, combine trips more effectively, or use your car less. Planning round trips with more than one stop often cuts the overall distance.

Use a Smaller, Less Expensive Vehicle

A smaller car is cheaper, handles better, is easier to park, and is less taxing on the environment. Conversely, an expensive new car would have such a high rate of depreciation that, once you own it, you would be tempted to drive it a lot to get your money's worth — even an average new domestic car depreciates about $4,000 annually, according to AAA.[1] An inexpensive used car will have a much lower rate of depreciation, plus if you don't drive much you may be able to save on insurance costs with a mileage-based insurance policy.

What Type of Vehicle?

- What is the car for? What capacity? Try to meet your usual needs, rather than the exceptional journeys.
- Small, light cars are more fuel-efficient.
- For in-town use, have a look at the electric car sources listed in the Resources section.
- To get the best fuel economy, choose a smaller engine (three- or four-cylinder, rather than V6, or V6 rather than V8)
- Fueleconomy.gov, run by the US Department of Energy, allows you to compare the efficiency of different car models.
- Consider buying, renting or borrowing a detachable trailer or large vehicle occasionally, rather than purchasing a larger car or SUV for occasional big loads.

Car Purchase Criteria

ConsumerReports.org provides well-researched, independent analysis of new and used car models, but much of the information is inaccessible without a subscription.

Edmunds.com is a for-profit alternative, which also offers information on ownership and driving costs. *Edmunds' New Cars & Trucks Buyer's Guide* and *Edmunds' Used Cars & Trucks Buyer's Guide* are available in bookstores throughout the US and Canada.

Below is a list of things to consider if you do decide to buy a car:

- Look at whole-life costs, such as price, fuel efficiency, financing, maintenance, repairs, depreciation and taxes. Also, look at each mode's expected reliability.
- Vehicles with automatic transmission use more fuel than those with manual shifting.

Sport-utility vehicles, pickup trucks and minivans accounted for over 40% of all vehicles sold in the US during the first half of 1995. These vehicles reportedly achieve as little as 10 mpg in stop-and-go traffic.[2]

- Compare total annual costs for various models. The AAA pamphlet, "Your Driving Costs 2005," provides averages for new domestic cars, calculated for 10,000, 15,000 and 20,000 miles per year.
- Look at fuel consumption figures — similar models of cars vary by over 25%.[3]
- Investigate insurance costs.
- Beware of the EPA fuel-economy ratings stickered on new cars. *Consumer Reports* has found a large

discrepancy between claimed and actual fuel efficiency. On average, vehicles produced in 2003 had mpg overstated by 30 percent.

- Remember that a high-visibility paint color is safest for pedestrians and cyclists.
- Information on alternative vehicles and fuels is available from the Alternative Fuels Data Center (Eere.energy.gov/afdc/), as well as from other organizations listed in the Resources section.

40–55 mph is the most economical driving speed. At 75 mph you use up to 30% more fuel than at 50 mph.[4]

Be Safe — Slow Down

Avoid rush hour when possible. Gas consumption doubles when speed drops from 30 mph to 10 mph. Also, stop-and-go traffic uses more gas than traveling at a constant speed.[5]

The "time saved by speeding" calculator estimates that for every ten minutes of driving at 65 mph instead of 55 mph, you only save 1 minute 14 seconds.[6] Is that worth the risk of accident or the possibility of getting a ticket?

- Avoid heavy acceleration and hard breaking.

- Lower speeds are crucial: excessive and inappropriate speed contributes to one third of all crashes. Every 1-mph drop in speed reduces crashes by 3% to 6%.[7]

Survival and Speed[8]

Vehicle Speed (mph)	<10	10–20	20–30	30–40	60
Pedestrian/Cyclist's Survival Chances	very good	95%	55%	15%	almost no chance

Join the Right Auto Club

"A lot of people belong to AAA because they think it's a nice place to get Triptiks and traveler's checks," says Daniel Becker, director of Sierra Club's global warming and energy program. "What they don't know is that AAA is a lobbyist for more roads, more pollution, and more gas guzzling."

There's now an excellent alternative. Launched in 2002 by business-savvy progressives, Better World Club offers nationwide (US) roadside assistance and the other services that you're used to getting from AAA. Membership includes eco-travel services, discounts on hybrid cars, insurance services, free maps, auto maintenance discounts and bicycle roadside assistance. The club offers mileage-based auto insurance, which is really a money saver for those who don't drive a great deal. Membership prices start at $54/year (2006), generally cheaper than AAA. See Betterworldclub.com/competition/ aaa.htm. At the time of writing, the club does not serve Canada. Better World donates 1% of its revenues to environmental causes. The club is even endorsed by Tom and Ray Magliozzi (aka Click and Clack), hosts of the Car Talk radio talk show. For further information, contact them toll-free in the US at 1 (866) 238-1137, or online at Betterworldclub.com.

Use Energy Efficiently

With fuel prices at historic highs, you can use a number of strategies to save gasoline. The most effective, of course, is to choose a fuel-efficient car and drive less.

- Reduce the number of your short trips, as a cold car engine produces more emissions, uses more fuel, and suffers more wear than when warm.
- Use the smallest, lightest vehicle available for the job
- Reduce drag by removing a trailer or roof rack and shutting windows and the sunroof. Remove any excess weight.
- Plan your trips in advance. Start the engine only when ready to go, and set off immediately. Avoid revving up, and push in a manual choke as soon as possible.
- Drive lightly and smoothly — heavy feet wear out brake pads and tires. Remember that aggressive driving increases fuel consumption by over 25%, and that pulling away too fast uses 60% more fuel.

For every 1 mph driven over 55 mph, the average vehicle loses approximately 2% in fuel economy. If everyone observed a speed limit of 55 mph, the US would save 4 million gallons of gasoline each day.[9]

- Get in the right gear: higher gears are more energy-efficient.
- Avoid unnecessary idling (anything over 45 seconds).

Automatic transmission can add 10–15% to fuel use, and air conditioning uses an average 15% more fuel.[10]

Maintenance

- Check your tires monthly. A 7-psi under-inflation wastes half a gallon of gasoline per tank.[11]
- Have your car serviced at least every year, or each 10,000 miles, to ensure the engine is properly tuned. Get the emissions and the catalytic converter checked at the same time.
- You should beware of devices that promise better fuel economy. *Consumer Reports* has repeatedly tested such products over the years and has not found any that actually work.[12]

- British motorists, however, report a savings of 5–20% on gasoline when using a Motoflow magnet (produced by Ecoflow, Simplymagnetic.com). They also recommend Ecotek's CB-26P fuel saver (Ecotek plc.com). Ecotek also sells a de-coking foam called PowerBoost to make older engines cleaner and more efficient.[13]
- Streamlining kits and aerodynamic styling cut can also fuel bills.

Cleaner, Greener Cars

The auto manufacturers sometimes claim that for environmental reasons it is best to buy a new, cleaner car and discard your old one. This assumes your previous car is now off the road, when more likely it's been resold and is still being driven around by someone else. (That's two cars on the road instead of one!) Secondly, a large share of a car's environmental impact, over its lifetime "from cradle to grave," takes place in the mining of materials to make the car, the manufacture, and the disposal. The actual driving of the car is just 40–60% of the total impact.[14] So car-caused pollution cannot be fully addressed by switching to alternative fuel sources or solar-charged car batteries; car ownership itself is an environmental problem.

Biofuels (ethanol, biodiesel, etc.) certainly have a role to play, but are not panaceas. They must go hand in hand with cutting our car use and our dependence on long-distance goods transport. According to one study we would need to convert a quarter of the planet's existing above-ground plant matter into biofuels — every year — to replace fossil fuels entirely.[15] Environmentalists such as Lester Brown of Earth Policy Institute warn of a future in which supermarkets and service stations compete for the same commodities. "If the food value of a commodity is less than the fuel value, it will be converted into fuel," he writes.[16]

Yet some biofuel crops show real promise. The jatropha tree, for example, can produce up to 15 kg of oil-rich seeds three times a year, can be grown on marginal land, produces seeds for up to 30 years, and its biodiesel fuel emits about 15% the CO_2 of petro-diesel. Jatropha (see Jatropha.de) is highly pest-resistant, helps to control erosion and provides a lucrative crop for former tobacco growers (thus not replacing a food crop). Sugarcane ethanol from Brazil can yield eight times the energy used to produce it, and can be made for $0.60 per gallon. Since sugarcane plant waste is burned to provide the heat for distilling, fossil fuel inputs are minimised (except in transporting the fuel to the consumer). The energy content of the fuel is about 67% that of gasoline, while biodiesel provides 90% of the energy of petro-diesel.[17]

Other crops fare worse. Oil palm, for example, is extremely destructive but will nonetheless be widely exploited for biodiesel because it's by far the cheapest source. Oil palm yields 508 gallons per acre, more than twice the yield of its closest rival, the coconut. (Jatropha yields 202 gallons per acre.) Friends of the Earth estimates that oil palm is already responsible for 87% of the deforestation in Malaysia.[18] Now that the European Union has decided that 5.75% of its transport fuel must come from plant sources by 2010, most of the remaining forest is threatened. To meet the projected European demand, 6 million hectares of forest are scheduled for clearance in Malaysia, and 16.5 million hectares in Indonesia. Oil palm biodiesel is even more destructive than crude oil from Nigeria, some critics claim.[19]

When making decisions about "greener" car purchase or alternative fuels, consider the following points:

- Buying a new car makes the buyer responsible for a greater part of its overall environmental impact than if he or she had bought the car later in its lifecycle. Also, buying a new car encourages more cars to be built, and enriches an industry that lobbies for more highways and car-based infrastructure. From an environmental and money-saving standpoint, it is generally better to buy a used car, even if its fuel efficiency is lower than that of a new car. You can make up the difference by driving the car less often, or by converting or modifying it to run more cleanly.
- Electricity use is not benign. The environmental impact depends on the fuel source of the power plant, whether natural gas, coal, nuclear, wind, hydro or solar. Electricity, however, tends to be much cheaper than gasoline.
- The impact of running cars on hydrogen would depend on the energy source used to separate water into pure hydrogen, as well as the impact of transporting it to the consumer. Hydrogen is more of a storage medium (like a battery) than an actual fuel. It would probably be more efficient to have cars run by natural gas than to burn natural gas to "produce" hydrogen and then burn the hydrogen in a car.
- If you're set on buying a new car, consider a hybrid such as the Toyota Prius, which can be converted (by, among others, a nonprofit group called CalCars in Palo

Alto), to run on electricity alone. Ron Gremban of CalCars reports that before the conversion, his Prius got 40–45 mpg and now it gets 65–100 mpg.[20]

- Americans who buy hybrid cars may be eligible for a tax credit of up to $3,150.[21]
- However, in terms of gas mileage, an efficient non-hybrid car such as the Smart (50–60 mpg) or the VW Beetle (especially with a drag reducer)[22] can easily rival a hybrid car, while having a lower sticker price.
- Whatever you do, don't start driving more once you have bought a "clean" car, justified by the eco-credentials or the savings at the pump. The extra driving will easily cancel out the difference.
- "Clean fuels" can be 50% more fuel efficient than standard gasoline.[23] Diesel is 30% more fuel-efficient than gasoline, but has a worse impact on human health.[24] Biodiesel is cleaner than ordinary diesel, but can be difficult to obtain. A map and list of US distributors are at Biodiesel.org/buyingbiodiesel/distributors/.
- For city driving, new compressed air engines are cleanest, and have a range of 120 miles. See the website Theaircar.com about the MDI City C.A.T. and for news of when it will be in production.
- There's enough used vegetable oil out there to fuel up perhaps .1/400th of our current vehicle fleet. Veggieavenger.com tells you how to take advantage of this underused resource.

SUCCESS STORY

For Rob Woodman, director of the Davis Pain Clinic in Davis, California, cars always represented wealth and masculinity, and his youth was spent repairing and driving cars. After high school, he always had a car, no matter how thin his finances got. Once establishing his psychology practice, he drove 35 minutes to his office in Sacramento every day for 15 years. But as increased traffic lengthened his commute and he became more conscious about pollution and oil dependence, he decided to move his practice closer to home. Though it took time to get re-established, the change has much improved his quality of life. His "commute" is now a relaxing four-minute walk. Rob now lives and works in Village Homes, a neighborhood of passive-solar homes, curving narrow lanes and open space. To emphasize public life and active transportation, homes are oriented toward common areas that include an extensive system of walking/cycling paths, as well as a variety of landscaped and garden areas, play structures, fruit and nut trees, vineyards and flowing creeks, all maintained by committees of residents. Rob and his patients greatly enjoy this beautiful setting and its community-minded atmosphere.

6

Living Without a Car

Planning is vital to success. Look at your lifestyle. Is it feasible to give the car up completely? Can you travel less or do things differently? Do you have everything you need to replace your car? If you've decided to take the plunge, here are some tips:

Before You Sell Your Car

Before you decide to get rid of your car, discuss being carfree with the others in your household. Below are some points to consider and/or discuss:

- Add up your car costs compared to the alternatives, using the table in the front of this book.
- Begin testing alternatives and restructuring your schedules.
- Research and plan how you will make your most frequent trips. Identify your nearest public transportation stops and stations, connections and last services, and where to securely park your bicycle.
- Consider buying a folding bicycle.
- Identify the weakest stage or link in your journey and work out how to deal with it.

- Work out the easiest walking and cycle routes with low curbs and gentle gradients. For cycling routes, you can plan your route to avoid busy left turns.
- Discover your local bike routes, walking paths and trails. Information is available from your city council, county government, parks and recreation office or tourist information center.
- Get any maps or transit schedules you might need. Some online map sources include Multimap.com, Mapquest. com, and Maps.google.com.
- Contact your nearest rental car company or car sharing club about occasional rental or club membership.
- Choose a specific date to get rid of your car.

Making it Work

Keep in mind that the early days will be the most difficult.

- Avoid places where cars predominate. For example, explore local amenities instead of out-of-town developments.
- Keep reminding yourself what you are gaining.
- Use the cash you've saved for treats to reward all those involved.
- Cash in on being carfree by renting out a parking place, driveway or garage, or converting a garage into a room to rent.
- For a list of the US cities best suited for carfree living, see Bikesatwork.com/carfree/. Canadian cities are not listed, but most would generally score better.

- If all else fails, move to Venice — Italy's famous and beautiful carfree city. There you'll have no need for a book such as this! Other carfree cities in the world, most of them dating back to medieval or pre-medieval times, are listed at Carfree.com/carfree_ places.html.

Sharing the Load

There are many things you can do to reduce the loads you carry.

- For groceries or other shopping, consider using a delivery service, or share a car for occasional trips.
- Only take or buy as much as you need and can carry.
- Ask others to help, or take loads for you. If appropriate, offer to pay them.
- Leave belongings in luggage lockers or other lockable storage, where available. Lockers can also be used for cycling gear.
- Rent or borrow a bike trailer, use a bicycle courier, or use a taxi, car or van, and do all your bulky jobs in one go.

Weather

Cold, wet or windy weather can be off-putting. So:

- Buy the best modern lightweight, thermal, waterproof and protective clothing that you can afford. Wear layers. You may also need an umbrella and waterproof bag.
- Carry or keep spare clothes at work to change into if needed.

- Choose sheltered (e.g., tree-lined) routes if possible.
- In really bad weather, get a taxi or share a ride.

Equipment

The right equipment can also make a big difference:

- Buy collapsible, lightweight and durable equipment.
- Consider buying two copies of a heavy book or two sets of tools, for example, if you would otherwise need to carry such items back and forth. This will allow you to leave one at home and one at work/school.

Carrying Loads

- Spread weight evenly. Use a durable backpack with back padding and padded shoulder straps for comfort.
- Push or pull a trailer, handcart, garden cart, stroller, wheeled suitcase, or the like.

- On a bike, use baskets, panniers or a trailer, or walk a bike with heavy loads in a basket, panniers or on both handlebars.
- Unless you have a trailer, a combination of medium-sized rear panniers, medium-sized panniers mounted low on the front, and a small handlebar bag is the best way to carry loads on a bike. The heavier the object, the lower it should be placed. Some front baskets detach to become bags.
- Trailer manufacturers are listed in this book's directory.
- Cycles Maximus specializes in load-carrying tricycles. Many trailers detach from bikes to become handcarts. Consider using child-carrying trailers for other loads.
- If you want to take the dog on a longer trip, try a dog trailer or a child trailer.

SUCCESS STORY

Sonya Newenhouse and Rebecca Grossberg of Madison, Wisconsin, already biked to work regularly, and wanted to see how they could further reduce their car dependence. In 2001, Sonya took a six-week trial separation from her car and discovered how easy it was. She only needed her car twice and learned that buses weren't just for commuting, but could bring her to her sister's house across town. This successful separation led her to "divorce" her car — and with the money saved, she's buying art. Rebecca also sold her car, and joined a bike trailer co-op so she could transport larger items, such as a broken television and computer to a recycling drop-off center. She got studded bike tires so she can ride comfortably through Wisconsin's icy winters. Through their consulting company, Madison Environmental Group, Sonya and Rebecca organize a two-week Carfree Challenge every September to motivate others to go on a car diet. The hope is that after the challenge, participants will continue to eliminate at least one car trip per week, reducing their CO_2 emissions by hundreds of pounds per year. Madison Environmental Group has also launched a car-sharing service.

Carrying Children

- Take public transit and keep the children entertained while someone else does the driving.
- Bike trailers offer good weather protection, and are stable and easy to pull.

- On a bike, use a child seat or trailer.
- Older children can pedal with you on a trailer bike, particularly good for 4- to 7-year-olds.
- Tricycles or tandems are good for family cycling.
- Some school "walking school bus" programs use handcarts or garden carts for carrying heavy school-bags.

7

Carfree Places

So far this book has been about personal choices and individual initiative. But readers of this book are surely not among those most responsible for today's auto-oriented town and cities, and their low-density, sprawl-based development pattern. So why put the onus on the individual, when even the most ardent motorists would be glad to leave their cars behind to visit a place such as Venice, Italy, where they get the full advantages of being carfree?

In Venice, for example, people can experience the intimacy of a human-scaled environment, with narrow streets, rich architectural detail, cleaner air, peace and quiet, and the ability to reach your destinations quickly and easily on foot. People can let their children wander freely, run around and play in the street without worrying about dangerous traffic. Many of these qualities, and the charm that they collectively provide, would be lost if even 1% of trips in Venice were by car, or if just 1% of Venetians parked cars in the city's streets. We must accept that some freedoms are mutually exclusive — we must choose on a place-by-place basis whether we offer the freedom to drive, or the freedom to have carfree streets.

To help us decide which freedom we prefer, we need more carfree urban places, so people can experience them, compare them side by side with auto-oriented places, and vote with their feet and their dollars — choosing which environment they prefer to live and work in.

In Europe, carfree housing developments already exist in London, Edinburgh, Amsterdam, Munich, Hamburg, Vienna, Freiburg, and Bern.[1] Other cities, such as Copenhagen and Nurenberg, have created a network of pedestrian streets, and converted parking lots into public squares.[2]

Closer to home, a number of pedestrian streets have been built over the past decades in the US and Canada — some have proved very successful (such as Church Street in Burlington, VT), others have not. We must learn from the ones that did it right. It's also important to build mixed-use carfree areas — with a combination of homes, businesses and non-commercial destinations — not just outdoor shopping malls.

A nonprofit group called CarFree City, USA is aiming to work with developers to convert disused urban "brownfield" sites into carfree human habitats. They conducted a study that calculated a savings of $915 million in building a carfree development of 12,000 residents vs. a typical suburban development of the same population.[3] And JH Crawford has written a book called *Carfree Cities*, describing how we could, and why we should, build entire cities carfree. The ultimate success of these efforts will depend on people making their demands known, and joining or initiating local carfree projects. This could start happening sooner than you think, assisted by efforts to avoid paying high gasoline costs, reduce emissions, encourage exercise, and reduce dependence on dwindling fossil fuel supplies.

As we put this book to press, North America's first major virtually carfree development, called Quarry Village, is being planned in Hayward, California, and is seeking buyers and renters. The Quarryvillage.org website provides a wealth of information that could be used to plan a similar project elsewhere.

- If you want to live in a carfree community, you'll need some way of doing outreach to find like-minded people in your area. There are online "carfree meet-up" groups for 15 different North American cities: Carfree. meetup.com.
- Reading the book *Carfree Cities* by J.H. Crawford, or reading the website Carfree.com are good ways to familiarize yourself with a very thoroughly researched vision of the concept.
- An excellent guidebook for municipalities is *Car-Free Development* by Lloyd Wright, available free online at Worldcarfree.net/resources/free.php.
- See the list of carfree places at Carfree.com/carfree_ places.html.
- Click on the "Register" tab at Carfreecity.us to complete a survey registering your interest in carfree living.
- The Towards Carfree Cities conference series has been held since 1997. It is now an annual five-day event, alternating between Europe and the Americas. For more information see Worldcarfree.net/conference/.

==

============ *SUCCESS STORY* ============

Toby Weymiller grew up in Seattle in a typical American multi-car family. As soon as he turned 16, he and his friends got their driver's licenses and drove everywhere they went. Toby went on to play college football and was living the American dream until a knee injury forced him onto a stationary bike. After the second day of staring at a blank wall while pedaling, he bought a real bicycle and began cycling all over town. After college, Toby lived carfree in Japan, where he was amazed to see a mass transportation system that really works. When he moved back to Seattle, he collided with the car culture of his youth. Although he stayed strong and continued to use mass transit, his bicycle and his feet, Seattle's transit system just wasn't as complete or convenient as Japan's. A few times a month, Toby needed a car, so he begged and borrowed from friends and family, with insurance concerns always coming up. Finally, Toby heard about a local car sharing company and enthusias-tically signed up. Toby's occasional transportation problem was solved, and the car sharing company paid for the gasoline, parking and maintenance — as well as for that pesky insurance.

8

Talking to Your Employer

Your employer may be unaware of the various possibilities that can help you to drive less — a variety of tools and programs described by the term "commuter choice." These are further broken down into four categories: mode choice, time choice, route choice and location choice.

Greener transportation brings financial and many other benefits to everyone. The company can save on parking expenses, take advantage of government tax breaks, improve on attracting and retaining employees, demonstrate its environmental credentials, and increase staff productivity, while reducing on-the-job stress.

Commuterchoice.com offers comprehensive information and resources for employers and commuters on workplace mobility management. The site includes local information for 18 US cities, and a link to the US Federal Highway Administration's "Commuter Choice Primer: An Employer's Guide to Implementing Effective Commuter Choice Programs."

Some of the options suggested by Commuter Choice include:

- Transportation information distribution; for example, this book, transit maps and schedules, etc.
- A carpooling database, preferential parking and financial incentives.

- Telecommuting, part-time work, job sharing and flex-time. For a fee, you can download a proposal template on one of these topics from Workoptions.com, fill in the blanks and submit it to your employer for consideration.
- Changing shift times to better match transit schedules.
- Compressed work weeks, allowing you to work, for example, a 4/40 plan (one weekday off every week by working four ten-hour days) or a 9/80 plan (one weekday off every two weeks by working nine nine-hour days per two-week period).
- Parking or company car cash out — commuters who are offered subsidized parking or a company car are sometimes offered the cash equivalent if they use alternative modes of transportation.
- Interest-free loans for a bicycle or transit pass.
- Discounts/subsidies on public transportation — US employers get tax deductions if they pay for their employees to commute by transit or vanpool, up to a limit of $100/month.
- Guaranteed ride home — commute using an alternative form of transportation and become eligible for a free taxi ride home in case of emergency or the need to work late.
- On-site showers, lockers and changing facilities.
- Pedestrian-friendly initiatives, such as traffic calming, crosswalks and low curbs.
- Cycling initiatives such as secure and conveniently located bike racks, company-owned folding bikes,

mileage-based travel allowances, and a bike fleet for work/breaks. Some bike shops may rent bikes to companies, and offer maintenance contracts for them.

- On-site facilities, such as a kitchen, cafeteria, nursery and ATM machine, to reduce the need for car travel during working hours.

Workplace Car Sharing Clubs

Many employers offer a fleet of cars for business trips. There are other options:

- They could convert this to a car sharing club to make vehicles available to staff for off-hours use.
- The car fleet could be operated by an independent car sharing club, with local businesses cooperating to make the program more viable.
- The company could become a corporate member of a car sharing club, and block-book vehicles during business hours with vehicles parked on-site.

- A small company or self-employed person could register staff with a car sharing club for both work and personal use.

Workplace car sharing clubs reduce commuting by car. They cut parking pressure at the workplace and can help ease rush hour traffic. The idea hasn't been widely implemented yet in North America, but lots of information is available from Carplus in the UK (Carclubs.org.uk).

9

Getting Active

Things You Can Do

- This book's directory contains listings of worthy nonprofit organizations that you can join and support. For a more extensive list, search the Carfree Green Pages: Worldcarfree.net/greenpages/.
- Urge your local government to implement traffic calming, improve public transportation service, and allocate a larger share of road space to cycling and walking.
- Promote World Carfree Day on September 22 each year, National Bike Month in May, and International Walk to School Day in October.
- Help form a local group of people who want to live in a carfree area, then approach investors and developers with your idea. Contact CarFree City, USA for guidance.
- Discuss Commuter Choice with your employer, using the information available on Commuterchoice.com.
- Join a carpool program run by your school, company or local government.

- If you're a parent, help your child's school to implement a Safe Routes to School program. See Walktoschool-usa.org for help.
- Start up or support a bicycle-based business, such as a delivery service or pedicab company.

10

The Rebound Effect

When cutting our car use, it's important to understand that our reduced environmental impact can be partially or entirely offset by increased impacts elsewhere in society, or even in our own behavior. In congested conditions, for example, traffic tends to expand or contract to fill the available road space – so the space freed up by some people who stop driving is quickly filled by other people who increase their driving.[1] And increases in fuel efficiency tend to be cancelled out by an increase in miles (or kilometers) driven. Similarly, someone who doesn't own a car will often do something else of similar impact, such as taking international vacations via airplane or buying a big house.

Therefore we must work to ensure that road space is permanently reallocated from motorized traffic to other modes, with techniques such as "road dieting," and that we seek to minimize our personal environmental impact by spending our income on labor-intensive goods and services rather than resource-intensive ones. Even if we do spend our money responsibly, the money quickly circulates into the hands of those who are less ethically motivated. Ultimately, a drop in GDP is the only way for North American society as a whole to reduce its impact. Voluntary simplicity will provide benefits to those who pursue it, but will not affect the society's overall level of consumption. Positive alternatives to economic growth are now being explored. In some countries, this is a debate that's out in the public consciousness, a growing debate that's being discussed seriously all the way up to the corridors of power.

Resources

This directory contains useful contacts, companies, organizations and resources, divided into the following categories:

- **Advocacy Organizations** – bicycle and pedestrian groups, carfree support groups
- **Alternative Cars & Fuels** – drive yourself cleaner
- **Automobile Clubs** – roadside service (even for bikes!), mileage-based insurance, free maps
- **Bicycles & Equipment** – bike trailers, electric bikes, folding bikes, pedicabs and work bikes
- **Books** – read more about automobile dependence and the alternatives
- **Car Pooling & Car Sharing** – community-oriented transportation solutions
- **Conferences & Events** – Bicycle Film Festival, Pro Bike/Pro Walk, World Carfree Day
- **Inter-City Buses & Trains** – Amtrak, Greyhound and other services less known
- **Local & Regional Transportation** – public transportation and trip planner websites for major metropolitan areas, online maps and direction
- **Magazines** – selected cycling and carfree periodicals
- **Telecommuting** – work from home and avoid the traffic
- **Web Sites & Listservs** – online resources and discussion

Advocacy Organizations

There are (fortunately!) too many groups out there to list here. However, you can search the Carfree Green Pages Worldcarfree.net/greenpages/ for your local organizations. For bicycle and pedestrian advocacy, below we list only national and international groups. We do however list local carfree groups and others of particular interest.

America Walks – A national coalition of local advocacy groups promoting walkable communities, assisting community pedestrian groups and educating the public. Old City Hall, 45 School Street, 2nd Floor, Boston, MA 02108, USA; phone: (617) 367-1170; e-mail: info@americawalks.org; website: Americawalks.org

Association for Commuter Transportation – An association for professionals who specialize in commute options and for everyone interested in creating a more workable transportation system. 1401 Peachtree Street, Suite 440, Atlanta, GA 30309, USA; phone: (678) 916-4940; website: Tmi.cob.fsu.edu/act/

Auto-Free New York – A movement wishing to "devehicularize" New York, increase pedestrian space and invest in new transit options. One Washington Square Village, Apartment 5D, NYC 10012, USA; phone: (212) 475-3394; website: Auto-free.org

Auto-Free Ottawa – A local group of carfree people. 797 Somerset Street, Suite 103, Ottawa, ON K1R 6R3, Canada; phone: (613) 237-1549; website: Afo.sandelman.ca

Auto-Free Orange County – A volunteer environmental organization, promoting a carfree life, public transit and personal fitness. Box 338, Laguna Beach, CA 92652, USA; phone: (949) 452-1393; e-mail: AutoFreeOrangeCounty@cox.net; website: Auto-free.net

CarFree City, USA – A non-profit organization with a mission to promote carfree development. P.O. Box 2841, Berkeley, CA 94702, USA; phone: (510) 849-4412; website: Carfreecity.us

Carfree Meet-Up Groups – 16 groups of carfree people based in the US and Canada who meet up for discussions and activities. Cities include: Cleveland, Seattle, Boston and Toronto. website: Carfree.meet up.com

Car Free Pittsburgh – A group wanting to aid Pittsburghers with the transition to alternative transportation through education and events. e-mail: info@carfreepittsburgh.org; website: Carfreepittsburgh.org

----

Center for Livable Communities – An organization that helps local governments and community leaders be proactive in their land use and transportation planning. Local Government Commission, 1414 K Street, Suite 600, Sacramento, CA 95814, USA; phone: (916) 448-1198; e-mail: center@lgc.org; website: Lgc.org/center

City Repair – An organized group action that educates and inspires communities and individuals to creatively transform the places where they live. They facilitate artistic and ecologically oriented place-making. PO Box 42615, Portland, OR 97242, USA; phone: (503) 235-8946; e-mail: thecircle@cityrepair.org; website: City repair.org

Congress for the New Urbanism – The New Urbanism movement seeks to reform all aspects of real estate development and promote denser, walkable, mixed-use communities. 140 South Dearborn Street, Suite 310, Chicago, IL 60603, USA; phone: (312) 551-7300; e-mail: cnuinfo@cnu.org; website: Cnu.org

Conservation Law Foundation – A large New England environmental advocacy organization. Features several excellent publications on alternative transport and traffic calming, free via their website. These include: "Take Back Your Streets: How to Protect Communities from Asphalt and Traffic." 62 Summer Street, Boston, MA 02110-1016, USA; phone: (617) 350-0990; website: Clf.org

Human-Powered Vehicle Association – Promotes the development and technological improvement of human-powered vehicles in the US and Canada, via competitions, etc. P.O. Box 1307, San Luis Obispo, CA 93406-1307, USA; phone: (877) 333-1029; website: Hpva.us

Institute for Transportation & Development Policy (ITDP) – A leader in developing and implementing green transport policy in the developing world, as an alternative to the US model. Innovative projects in nearly every corner of the world. 115 West 30th Street, Suite 1205, New York, NY 10001, USA; phone: (212) 62912-8001; e-mail: mobility@itdp.org; website: Itdp.org

----

League of American Bicyclists – National education, advocacy and lobby group; sponsors National Bike Month and Bike-to-Work Day; quarterly magazine; website links to state/local US bike groups. 1612 K Street NW, Suite 800, Washington, DC 20006, USA; phone: (202) 822-1333; e-mail: bikeleague@bikeleague.org; website: Bikeleague. org

National Association of Railroad Passengers – Promotes intercity passenger rail service in the US. Offers fare discounts and information to train travelers. 900 – 2nd Street, NE, Suite 308, Washington, DC 20002, USA; phone: (202) 408-8362; e-mail: narp@narprail.org; website: Narprail.org

National Center for Bicycling and Walking – Supports the activities and initiatives of people working to make America a better place to walk and ride a bicycle. Website has some good practical online publications and resources for cycling and pedestrian advocates. 8120 Woodmont Avenue, Suite 650, Bethesda, MD 20814, USA; phone: (301) 656-4220; e-mail: info@bikewalk.org; website: Bike walk.org

Noise Pollution Clearinghouse – Information and links on noise pollution. P.O. Box 1137, Montpelier, VT 05601-1137, USA; phone: (888) 200-8332; website: Nonoise.org

Partnership for a Walkable America – A national coalition of governmental agencies and non-profit organizations working to improve the conditions for walking in America and to increase the number of people who walk regularly. website: Walkableamerica.org

Pedestrian and Bicycle Information Center – This center provides information for anyone interested in pedestrian and bicycle issues, including planners, engineers, private citizens, advocates and educators. 730 Airport Road, Suite 300, Campus Box 3430, Chapel Hill, NC 27599-3430, USA; phone: (919) 962-2203; e-mail: pbic@pedbikeinfo.org; website: Pedbikeinfo.org

Project for Public Spaces – Works with local groups and authorities to establish healthy public spaces, often by taking space away from car infrastructure. 153 Waverly Place, 4th Floor, New York, NY 10014, USA; phone: (212) 620-5660; e-mail: pps@pps.org; website: Pps.org

Surface Transportation Policy Project (STPP) – US national lobby group that advocates for sustainable transportation. Publishes many useful reports and newsletters, most of which are available for free on its website. 1100 – 17th Street NW, 10th Floor, Washington, DC 20036, USA; phone: (202) 466-2636; e-mail: stpp@transact.org; website: Transact.org

Trails and Greenways Clearinghouse – A project of Rails-to-Trails Conservancy, that provides technical assistance and information to trail and greenway advocates and developers across the nation. 1100 17th Street NW, 10th Floor, Washington, DC 20036, USA; phone: (877) 476-9297; e-mail: greenways@railtrails.org; websites: Trails andgreenways.org, Railtrails.org; see also website: Americantrails. org

Transport 2000 Canada – A non-profit organization who promotes environmentally-sound transportation solutions in Canada. website: Transport2000.ca

Thunderhead Alliance – The national coalition of state and local bicycle and pedestrian advocacy organizations working to break down the barriers to safe bicycling and walking. P.O. Box 3309, Prescott, AZ 86302, USA; phone: (928) 541-9841; e-mail: Info@Thunderhead Alliance.org; website: Thunderheadalliance.org

Victoria Transport Policy Institute – Independent research organization dedicated to developing innovative and practical tools for solving transportation problems. Provides a wide range of studies, guides and software, most available free on its website. 1250 Rudlin Street, Victoria, BC, V8V 3R7, Canada; phone: (250) 360-1560; e-mail: info@vtpi.org; website: Vtpi.org

Walkable Communities, Inc. – Organized to help communities become more walkable and pedestrian friendly. Offers presentations, walkable audits, training courses, workshops, and more. Has many online resources, as well as publications, videotapes, slide sets and

----

photo CDs to assist in community education. 320 South Main Street, High Springs, FL 32643, USA; phone: (386) 454-3304; e-mail: walkable@aol.com; website: Walkable.org

World Carfree Network – Hub of the global carfree movement, with member organizations around the world and many international projects. Kratka 26, 100 00 Prague 10, Czech Republic; phone: +(420) 274-810-849; e-mail: info@worldcarfree.net; website: Worldcarfree.net

Alternative Cars & Fuels

Alternative Fuels Data Center – A vast collection of information on alternative fuels and the vehicles that use them. Run by the US Department of Energy. Also includes the National Alternative Fuels Hotline, a team of alternative fuel and advanced technology vehicle experts ready to provide the information you need. phone: (800) 423-1363 (hotline); e-mail: hotline@afdcweb.nrel.gov; website: Eere.energy.gov/afdc/

Biodiesel America/Veggie Van – Biodiesel is a fuel made from vegetable oil. See the website for the adventures of the Veggie Van which traveled 25,000 miles across the US during 1997 and 1998 using this fuel. 8033 Sunset Blvd 154, Hollywood, CA 90046, USA; phone: (310) 496-3292; website: Biodieselamerica.org

Electric Drive Transportation Association – An industry association dedicated to advancing vehicles powered by electricity with the aim of creating sustainable mobility. 1350 I Street, NW, Suite 1050,Washington, DC 20005-3305, USA; phone: (202) 408-0774; e-mail: info@electric drive.org; website: Electricdrive.org

MDI Air Car – A car designed to use compressed air technology to increase energy efficiency and reduce pollution. website: Theaircar.com

WestStart-CALSTART – A non-profit organization that works with the public and private sectors to develop advanced transportation technologies and foster companies that will help clean the air, lessen dependence on foreign oil, reduce global warming, etc. 48 South Chester Avenue,

Pasadena, California 91106, USA; phone: (626) 744-5600; e-mail: calstart@calstart.org; website: Calstart.org

Zero Air Pollution (ZAP) – Source for buying electric cars and electric vehicles of all kinds. Based in Santa Rosa, CA. phone: 800 (251)-4555; website: Zapworld.com

Automobile Clubs

American Automobile Association – Not the benign membership service organization that it appears. AAA works as part of the automobile and road lobby, pushing for more freeway construction, lower fuel-efficiency standards, and against strong action on climate change. However, "Driving Costs 2005" is a useful pamphlet on the average costs of owning a new domestic car. website: Aaanewsroom.net/ Files/Driving_Costs_2005.pdf.

Better World Club – Only environmentally friendly auto club in the US (does not serve Canada as of 2006). Provides nationwide roadside assistance for both cars and bicycles, as well as a host of other services. Offers mileage-based auto insurance. toll-free: (866) 238-1137; website: Betterworldclub.com

Canadian Automobile Association – Canada's equivalent of the AAA. Has 11 member clubs in 10 provinces and three territories, with 130 offices nationwide. website: Caa.ca

Bicycles & Equipment
Here you'll find listings of companies that produce bicycles and bicycle equipment that are of particular interest for utilitarian cycling. The section is further broken down into four categories: Bicycle Panniers & Trailers; Electric Bicycles; Folding Bicycles; and Pedicabs, Work Bikes & Special-Needs Bicycles.

Bicycle Panniers & Trailers
Panniers are the storage bags that attach to the sides of a front or rear rack. The other main storage option is a bike trailer. An eternal debate rages as to which is better. The US and Canada have more than a dozen quality trailer manufacturers. You may wish to start with thE bike trailer comparison chart: Bikeroute.com/ TrailerMatrix.htm.

B.O.B Trailers, Inc. – Manufactures two models of one-wheel, pod-shaped bike trailers for bike commuters and tourists. Carrying capacity: 70 lbs. Cost: $300–400. Also makes strollers and trailer accessories. Website includes "where to buy" section for the US and Canada, as well as for Internet and international sales. 3641 Sacramento Drive, #3, San Luis Obispo, CA 93401, USA; phone: (800) 893-2447; website: Bobtrailers.com

Burley Design Cooperative – Worker-owned manufacturer of bike trailers, tandems, recumbents, road bikes, commuter bikes, clothing and gear since 1978. Website includes "dealers" section for the US and Canada, as well as for Internet and international sales. 4020 Steward Road, Eugene, OR 97402, USA; phone: (541) 687-1644; toll-free: (866) 248-5634; website: Burley.com

Bikes At Work, Inc. – Manufactures several models of cargo bike trailers capable of carrying everything from a few bags of groceries to a refrigerator or a household of furniture. Sized to carry standard 18-gallon storage containers (such as Rubbermaid Roughtote), but also converts to flatbed. Three different lengths (32", 64" and 96" [81, 163, and 254 cm]). Carrying capacity: 300 lb (136 kg). Cost: $350–450. Pedicabs also available. Website includes a page that calculates your costs of car ownership, as well as a section of tips on carfree living. 129 Washington Avenue, Ames, IA 50010, USA; phone: (515) 233-6120; website: Bikesatwork.com

Bykaboose International – Manufactures two models of collapsible bike trailers. Carrying capacity: 100 lbs. with 4.5 cubic feet of cargo space. Comes with a fitted cover to keep your cargo dry in bad weather. Cost: approximately US$200. 814 Spruce Street, Deerfield, IL 60015, USA; phone: (847) 370-9978; toll-free: (800) 441-9163; e-mail: info@bykaboose.com; website: Bykaboose.com

BicycleR Evolution – Standard model trailer ("The Shopper") features a 24-gallon, watertight, lockable container that will hold four large paper grocery bags, full to the brim, plus whatever you attach on top. "Heavy Duty Trailer" model holds six grocery bags. Hitch fits all bikes, and attaches and releases in seconds. Disassembles with three thumb screws and fits inside its own box. Converts easily to flatbed trailer. Optional walking handle available. Cost: $150–250 plus shipping. 985 Irving Road, Eugene, OR 97404, USA; phone: (541) 517-2931; toll-free: (866) 821-9535; e-mail: info@bikerev.com; website: Bikerev.com

Blue Sky Cycle Carts – Since 1979. Basic trailer models come in Standard, Long, Wide and Long and Wide. Carrying capacity: 250-300 lbs. Cost: $250–360. Special model available for carrying physically handicapped passenger, offers front or rear facing seating position, and bucket seat or tall sling seat; can be fitted with a canopy and other accessories. Cost: $460–700. PO Box 5788, Bend OR 97708, USA; toll-free: (800) 669-1753; phone: (503) 383-7109; e-mail: sales@blueskycyclecarts.com; website: Blueskycyclecarts.com

Brule Mountain Gear – A supplier of bicycle panniers that convert into backpacks. P.O. Box 12, Aymler, PQ, J9H 5EA, Canada; phone: (819) 685-9163; toll free: (888) 430-7225; e-mail: info@panpack.com; website: Panpack.com

Cycle Tectonics, LLC – Manufactures the Quik-Pak X-Press, the "Conestoga wagon" of bike trailers. Larger and lighter than B.O.B. and Burley trailers. Collapsible frame with fabric cargo hold provides 10,000 cubic inches of storage space. Can be folded in an instant and carried like a suitcase. Carrying capacity: 75 lbs. Weight: 14 lbs. Cost: US$325. PO Box 470, Canon City, CO, 81215, USA; phone: (719) 269-7535; e-mail: ray@quik-pak.com; website: Quik-pak.com

CycleTote Corporation – "The Lexus of Bicycle Trailers." The family models are considered to be the safest child carriers on the market. Touring/utility trailers: $380–470. Family models: $430–475. Special Needs trailer: $920+. Weight: 16.5–34 lbs. Carrying capacity: 100–175 lbs.; 8,322–27,220 cubic inches. 517 No. Link Lane, Ft. Collins, CO 80524, USA; toll-free: (800) 747-2407; international phone: +1 (970) 482-2401; e-mail: cycletote@cycle tote.com; website: Cycletote.com

EQUINOX Tourlite – Bike trailer with lots of options. Converts to garden cart, Nordic ski sled, jogging trailer, canoe/kayak trailer, portable dog kennel, etc. Cost: $260–400. Many accessories and kits to choose from. Mail order from Cottage Grove, Oregon. Website not updated since 2002. toll-free: (800) 942-7895; phone: (541) 942-7895; e-mail: equinox@efn.org; website: Efn.org/~equinox

Jandd Mountaineering – A manufacturer of bicycle panniers and other useful equipment. Also caters for recumbent bikes. Their products come with a lifetime guarantee against material and manufacturer defects. 1345 Specialty Drive #D, Vista CA 92081, USA; phone: (760) 597-9021; website: Jandd.com

Koolstop International, Inc. – Two types of one-wheel touring trailers, four models of children's trailers, and one "Kargo Van" trailer for bulky cargo. Also makes jogging strollers. 1061 South Cypress Street, La Habra, CA 90632, USA; toll-free: (800) 586-3332; e-mail: ksi california@sbcglobal.net; website: Koolstop.com

Traileron – A bike trailer hitch designed to golf pull Radio Flyer-style wagons, portable folding/luggage carts, garden carts, beach carts, golf carts and dollies. Cost: US$20. e-mail: customerservice@traileron.com; website: Traileron.com

Ortlieb – A supplier of a wide range of high-end but waterproof panniers, bike messenger bags and other useful bicycle accessories. website: Ortlieb.com

Xtracycle Inc. – Convert your existing bike into a Sport Utility Bicycle with the Xtracycle "FreeRadical" kit. Imagine your favorite bike, with the rear wheel stretched out behind the seat, a big, stable platform for a load or a passenger, and expandable saddlebags on either side. Unlike with bike trailers, your bike is still lightweight and fast, and has great handling because the load is centered between your two wheels. 29085 Highway 49, North San Juan, CA 95960, USA; toll-free: (888) 537-1401; phone: (530) 292-1401; e-mail: info@xtra cycle. com; website: Xtracycle.com

Electric Bicycles

Cycle Electric International Consulting Group – Website strives to provide useful, reliable information for buyers, sellers, owners and "fixers" of LEVs (light electric vehicles). Provides a good overview of the options available. website: Electric-bikes.com

Currie Technologies, Inc. – The leading US manufacturer of electric scooters, also offers electric bikes, including a folding model. 20600 Nordhoff Street, Chatsworth, CA 91311, USA; toll-free: (800) 377-4532; phone: (818) 734-8123; website: Currietech.com

Electrik Motion – Manufacturers the LashOut electric bicycles and scooters. Base model starts at $800. Also offers electric golf carts. toll-free: (866) 372-6687; e-mail: sales@electrikmotion.com; website: Electrik motion.com

Electric Sierra Cycles – Manufacturers the Synergy Cycle electric-assist bicycle. Base model starts at US$800. phone: (831) 425-1593; e-mail: escuspd@attitude.com; website: Electricrecbikes.com

EV Global Motors Corporation – State-of-the-art electric bicycles from Lee Iacocca's new company. Available in 24- and 36-volt versions, plus a folding mini e-bike. 3631 Union Pacific Avenue, Los Angeles, CA 90023, USA; toll-free: (800) 871-4545; phone: (323) 266-3456; e-mail: info@evglobal.com; website: Evglobal.com

Vectrix – Producer of the Vectrix Electric Maxi-Scooter (available from 2006), which is designed to outperform gas-powered scooters. Top speed: 64 mph. Battery range: 68 miles (at a steady 30 mph). Hybrid fuel-cell version available. website: Vectrixusa.com

Zero Air Pollution (ZAP) – Source for buying electric scooters, bike kits, trikes, motorcycles and electric vehicles of all kinds. Based in Santa Rosa, CA. phone: 800 (251)-4555; website: Zapworld.com

Folding Bicycles

Bike Friday – Custom-made folding and tandem bikes, from US$800 to
$6,000+. 3364 West 11th Avenue, Eugene, OR 97402, USA; toll-
free: (800) 777-0258; phone: (541) 687-0487; website: Bikefriday.
com

Brompton – Quality British manufacturer of folding bikes. Cost: $850
–1,000+. US and Canadian dealers listed on website. website:
Bromptonbicycle.co.uk

Go Bike – A new entrant on to the folding bike scene from Canada. The
model uses a 20" wheel size. website: Legroupego.com

Go Go Bike – Folding bike collapses down in three easy steps, weighs
between 13–14 kg and comes with a carry bag for use on public
transportation. 2501 South Garnsey Street, Santa Ana, CA 92707,
USA; toll-free: (888) 498-GOGO; website: Gogobike.com

iXi Bike – A complete rethinking of the bicycle. Futuristic, stylish and
collapsible. Lightweight aluminum frame comes apart in seconds for
easy stowing and transporting. Grease-free belt drive system will
never stain your clothes. Delta Cycle Corp., 21 Cocasset Street,
Foxboro, MA 02035, USA; toll-free: (800) 474-6615; e-mail:
customerservice@ixibike.com; website: Ixibike.com

$999⁰⁰

Strida – A quality folding bike for just over $300, produced in the UK. Online
ordering available. website: Strida.com

Pedicabs, Work Bikes & Special-Needs Bicycles

Human Powered Machines – Small-scale manufacturer of a variety of work
bike models, as well as trailers and recumbents. 455 West 1st
Avenue, Eugene, OR 97401, USA; toll-free: (800) 343-5568;
phone: (541) 343-5568; website: Efn.org/~cat/html/sub_page_hmp
products.htm

Lightfoot Cycles – Industrial cargo bikes, pedicabs, electric- and gas-assist
bicycles, custom utility and special-needs bikes and trikes. toll-free:

(866) 821-4750; e-mail: info@lightfootcycles.com; website: Light
footcycles.com

Main Street Pedicabs, Inc. – Manufacturer of human-powered vehicles
including pedicabs (pedal powered taxis), pedal-electric rickshaws,
cargo trikes, and work bikes. 11811 Upham Street #9, Broomfield,
CO 80020, USA; phone (303) 295-3822; website: Pedicab.com

Organic Engines – Manufacturer of recumbent bikes and trikes, including the
"Sensible Utility Vehicle" (SUV), which comes in cargo trike and
pedicab versions. 1888 Mills Street, Tallahassee, FL, 32310, USA;
phone: (850) 224-7499; e-mail: kavanagh@tfn.net; website: Organic
engines.com

Step n' Go – Supplier of three-wheel, step-action, self-balancing cycles that
eliminate having to pedal. Offers alternatives for brake application,
etc. 6 Linden Terrace, Burlington, VT 05401, USA; toll-free: (800)
648-7335; e-mail: info@stepngo.com; website: Stepngo.com

Worksman Cycles – Since 1898. Manufacturer of bikes and trikes for work,
recreation and special needs. Even sells traditional New York street
corner hot dog trailer/push carts (minus the hot dogs)! 94–15 100th
Street, Ozone Park, NY 11416, USA; toll-free (888) 394-3353;
phone: (718) 322-2000; e-mail: cycles@worksman.com; websites:
Worksman.com (general info), Worksmancycles.com (prices),
800buycart.com (buy a cart)

Books

For further reading, consider the following titles: *For Love of the Automobile* by
Wolfgang Sachs, *The Geography of Nowhere* and *Home from Nowhere* by
James Howard Kunstler, *Carfree Cities* by J.H. Crawford, *Divorce Your Car!* by
Katie Alvord, *Asphalt Nation* by Jane Holtz Kay and *Life Between Buildings* by
Jan Gehl. *CARtoons* by Andy Singer and *Roadkill Bill* by Ken Avidor combine
seriousness with a comic approach. For children: *Family Mouse Behind the
Wheel, Alice in Underland* and *The Little Driver*. On oil depletion: *The Party's
Over: Oil, War and the Fate of Industrial Societies* by Richard Heinberg. All of
the above titles are carried by the following two online sources:

Detour's UrbanSource – Online source for books and resources on transportation and urban ecology. 850 Coxwell Avenue, 2nd Floor, Toronto, ON M4C 5R1, Canada; phone: (416) 338-5087; e-mail: info@detourpublications.com; website: Detourpublications.com

World Carfree Network Resource Centre – Online and mail-order source for books, videos, t-shirts, bike stickers and other products related to automobile dependence and the alternatives. Kratka 26, 100 00 Prague 10, Czech Republic; phone: +(420) 274-810-849; e-mail: orders@worldcarfree.net; website: Worldcarfree.net/resources/

Car Pooling & Car Sharing

Local carpooling information is often listed in your local telephone directory.

Carpool.ca and Carpooltool.com – Two Canadian carpooling sites where you can register to find a rideshare match. Free registration. website: Carpool.ca, Carpooltool.com

Carsharing.net – Provides a good explanation of car sharing and links to all existing car sharing programs in North America. "If you drive less than 12,000 km (7,500 miles) a year and you don't need a car for work every day, car sharing will likely save you thousands of dollars a year, give you greater mobility — and actually reduce pollution." website: Carsharing.net

ConnectorUSA – Vanpooling, also carpooling and car sharing. toll-free: (800) 826-7433; website: Vpsiinc.com

eRideShare.com – A free service for connecting commuters, or travelers going the same way. Most popular carpool and cross-country rideshare site in the US and Canada. By splitting fuel expense and tolls, you can travel 300 miles for about $10 in a 30-mpg vehicle, which is three to six times cheaper than Greyhound and Amtrak. Some drivers offer the ride for free, just for your charming company. "A 40-mile total daily commute costs about $2,600 per year. Ridesharing with one other person can save you $1,300. Double the figure for an 80-mile total daily commute." website: Erideshare.com

Flexcar – For-profit car sharing club in Chicago, Los Angeles, Portland, San Diego, San Francisco, Seattle, and Washington DC. Revolution, the investment company run by AOL co-founder Steve Case, owns the controlling share in Flexcar. website: Flexcar.com

Zipcar – For-profit, web-based, easy-to-use, car sharing club in Boston, Chapel Hill, Minneapolis, New York City, San Francisco, and Washington DC. Expanding to Atlanta, Austin, Chicago, Dallas, Miami, Philadelphia, Phoenix, Pittsburgh, Portland, Seattle, Toronto and Vancouver. Online application. You can compare the costs of car sharing vs. new car ownership at Zipcar.com/is-it/compare-own. toll-free: (866)   4-ZIP-CAR   (866-494-7227);   e-mail: info@zipcar.com; website: Zipcar.com

Conferences & Events

Bicycle Film Festival – The Bicycle Film Festival celebrates the bicycle in all its forms. Annual event takes place in a growing number of cities, including New York, Los Angeles, London, San Francisco and Tokyo. website: Bicyclefilmfestival.com

Critical Mass – Monthly community celebrations in which cyclists ride together in one big group and take back the streets. See these sites to find your nearest ride, or start your own! websites: Critical-mass.org, Criticalmassrides.info

International Walk to School Day – Each October children, parents, teachers across the globe walk to school to celebrate International Walk to School Day. See website to find out how you can get involved and for information about the Safe Routes to School programs. Partnership for a Walkable America, 730 Airport Road, Suite 300 / Campus Box 3430 Chapel Hill, NC 27599-3430, USA; phone: (919) 962-7419; website: Walktoschool-usa.org

National Bike Month – A whole month of events promoting the use of the bicycle including Bike to Work Week and Bike to Work Day. For information about these events, other activities and future dates see the League of American Bicyclists websites. websites: Bike league. org, Bikemonth.com

----

Pro Bike / Pro Walk Conference – Conference organized every two years by the National Center for Bicycling and Walking. 8120 Woodmont Avenue, Suite 650, Bethesda, MD 20814, USA; phone: (301) 656-4220; e-mail: info@bikewalk.org; website: www.bikewalk.org

Towards Carfree Cities conference series – Brings together people from around the world promoting practical alternatives to car dependence, with an emphasis on carfree areas and carfree cities. website: Worldcarfree.net/conference/

Velo Mondial conference series – An international cycling planning conference that brings together politicians, professionals and bicycle user representatives every four years. Velo City conferences held every two years. websites: Velomondial.net, Ecf.com/ networks/net_conferences1.htm

World Carfree Day – Each year on September 22, people from around the world gather to celebrate carfreedom and to demonstrate the alternatives. Although the "official" day is September 22 many cities hold activities all week or on another more convenient day (such as on the weekend). websites: Worldcarfree.net/wcfd/; 22september.org

Inter-City Buses & Trains

For other US services, see Apta.com/links/intercity.cfm. For other Canadian services see Apta.com/links/international/canada.cfm.

Acadian Lines – Operates buses throughout New Brunswick, Nova Scotia and Prince Edward Island, as well as a few towns in Quebec. 961 Main Street, Moncton, NB E1C 1G8, Canada; toll-free: (800) 567-5151; e-mail: info@acadianbus.com; website: Acadianbus.com

Alaska Railroad – Passenger trains in the 49th state. toll-free: (800) 544-0552 (outside Anchorage); phone: (907) 265-2494; e-mail: reservation@akrr.com; website: Akrr.com

Amtrak – Amtrak provides intercity passenger rail service to more than 500 destinations in 46 states on a 22,000-mile route system with 34 routes. For schedules, fares and information, passengers may call

(800) USA-RAIL [(800) 872-7245] or see Amtrak.com. See route map at end of this book.

Amtrak's regular passenger discounts are as follows (2006):

- Children aged 2–15 ride half-price every day
- Students save 15% with an ISIC or Student Advantage card
- Seniors: Amtrak travelers 62 years of age and over receive a 15% discount on the applicable adult rail fare on most Amtrak trains
- Veterans save 15% with a Veterans Advantage card
- National Association of Railroad Passengers (NARP) members save 10%
- AAA members save 10% when they use a AAA card

With online booking at Amtrak.com, you can find weekly specials with up to 90% off on selected routes. The site also features special advertised fares, such as group discounts, tour packages, etc.

Coach Canada – Provides scheduled bus service in Southeastern Ontario and Southern Quebec. Connections with third-party carriers extend service to New York City and other major North American locations. Professional charter service is also offered to groups of any size. 791 Webber Avenue, P.O. Box 4017, Peterborough, ON K9J 7B1, Canada; toll-free: (800) 461-7661; phone: (705) 748-6411; e-mail: schedules.canada@coachcanada.com; website: Coachcanada.com

Green Tortoise Adventure Travel – Very funky bus company offers sleeper coaches, good food, and stops at hot springs and such, on meandering tours to national parks and other tourist destinations throughout North America. Charters available. 494 Broadway, San Francisco, CA 94133 USA; phone (US outside SF Bay area and Canada): (800) 867-8647 or phone (Bay Area & Worldwide): (415) 956-7500; website: Greentortoise.com

Greyhound – The largest North American provider of inter-city bus transportation, serving more than 3,300 destinations with 17,000 daily departures across the continent. For schedules, fares and information, passengers may call (800) 231-2222 or see Grey hound.com. See route map at end of this book. Also provides

Greyhound PackageXpress (GPX). In Canada, contact (800) 661-TRIP (8747) or see Greyhound.ca (includes information, schedules and fares for routes served by Voyageur). Greyhound Mexico can be reached at (800) 710-8819 and Greyhound.com.mx.

Greyhound has the following every-day discounts (2006):

- Children ages 2–11 get a 40% discount.
- Students with a Student Advantage card ($20 from www.student advantage.com) save 15% on travel and 50% on Greyhound PackageXpress shipping.
- Seniors 62 and over get a 5% discount upon request.
- Military and Veteran discounts of 10–15% available.
- Tickets can be purchased online (Greyhound.com or Greyhound.ca), over the phone with a credit card [in US: (800) 231-2222; in Canada: (800) 661-8747], or at the terminal. Routes served by Voyageur can also be booked through Greyhound Canada.

Greyhound also offers a variety of advance purchase and unrestricted fares:

- *eSavers* – online specials to selected destinations.
- *Companion Fare* – Bring a companion (either a child or an adult) for 50% off when you buy one adult ticket at the regular walk-up price at least three days in advance of travel. Offer good for both one-way and round-trip tickets.
- *Go Anywhere Fares* – Travel for as low as $29 each way with a seven-day advance purchase. These are mileage-based fares, with nine categories from 1–300 miles ($29 one way) to over 2,800 miles ($109). Slightly higher rates apply for Friday and weekend travel.
- *Discovery Pass programs* – Five different passes for unlimited travel within a certain time period, ranging from 7 to 60 days. The Domestic Ameripass is for use throughout the US. The Domestic Canada Pass is for use throughout Canada. The Domestic North America CanAm Pass is for both countries. To complicate things further, there's also the Domestic Eastern CanAm Pass (Eastern US and Canada) and the Domestic West Coast CanAm Pass (Western US and Canada). Discoverypass.com, operated by Greyhound, has all the prices and details.

Jefferson Lines – Runs daily scheduled inter-city bus service in 11 states throughout America's Heartland, extending from Dallas to Winnipeg. Package delivery. Connections to Greyhound system. toll-free: (888) 864-2832; website: Jeffersonlines.com

Peter Pan Bus Lines – Operates 400 buses in the US Northeast, mainly in the corridor between Washington, DC, and Boston. Also serves Albany, NY and western Massachusetts. 1776 Main Street, Springfield, MA 01103, USA; toll-free: (800) 237-8747; phone: (413) 781-2900; website: Peterpanbus.com

Trailways Transportation System – A US-wide regionally based bus system that is comprised of privately owned and operated franchisees. Primarily serving passengers along the Eastern Seaboard, in the Southeast and Midwest. Also offers localized scheduled service in British Columbia and in the states of California, Montana, Oregon, Texas and Washington. "Schedules" page of website includes phone numbers and websites of franchisees, which usually have company names ending in the word "Trailways." website: Trailways.com

Vermont Transit Lines – Bus service links the major cities of New England with Boston, Montreal and New York City. Other daily services connect rural communities and colleges with larger cities within the states of Maine, Massachusetts, New York, New Hampshire and Vermont. Also offers connections between New England and Canada. Same-day package delivery within New England. 45 Pine Street, Burlington, VT 05401, USA; toll-free: (800) 642-3133 (in Vermont), (800) 451-3292 (out of state); website: Vermonttransit. com

VIA Rail – Canada's passenger train network. VIA Rail Canada runs more than 460 trains per week over a 14,000-kilometer network linking more than 450 localities in Canada. phone: (888) VIA RAIL (888-842-7245); website: Viarail.ca

Voyageur – Intercity bus services in Ontario and Quebec. See Greyhound (Greyhound.ca).

Local and Regional Transportation

American Public Transportation Association (APTA) represents the interests of North American transit agencies. Its website (www.apta.org) has links to every local, regional and inter-city public transportation service in North America.

For directions by car, to/from anywhere in the US or Canada, see Google Maps (Maps.google.com). Other map websites include Mapquest.com and Multi map.com.

Below are web addresses of public transportation information and web-based trip planning software for the 25 largest metropolitan areas in the United States, and the top 10 metropolitan areas in Canada. They are listed in order of metropolitan area population size, by country.

UNITED STATES:

New York City – Mta.info; Trips123.com

Los Angeles – Metro.net; Metrolinktrains.com

Chicago – Rtachicago.com

Washington, DC – Wmata.com

San Francisco, San Jose, Oakland – 511.org; Transit.511.org/tripplanner/

Philadelphia – Septa.org

Boston – Mbta.com

Detroit – Ci.detroit.mi.us/ddot/

Dallas – Dart.org

Houston – Ridemetro.org

Atlanta – Itsmarta.com (trip planner in beta at 205.152.13.212/tripplanner/)

Miami – Co.miami-dade.fl.us/transit/

Seattle – served by four regional transit companies, each with its own trip planner: Metro Transit (Transit.metrokc.gov), Pierce Transit (Pierce transit.org), Community Transit (Commtrans.org) and Sound Transit (Soundtransit.org)

Phoenix – Valleymetro.org

Minneapolis-St. Paul – Metrotransit.org

Cleveland – Gcrta.org

San Diego – Sdcommute.com

St. Louis – Metrostlouis.org (no trip planner)

Denver – Rtd-denver.com

Tampa – Hartline.org

Pittsburgh – Portauthority.org

Portland, OR – Trimet.org

Cincinnati – Sorta.com (no trip planner)

Sacramento – Sacrt.com; Sacregion511.org
Kansas City – Kcata.org

CANADA:
Toronto – City.toronto.on.ca/ttc/ (no trip planner); regional info:
    Gotransit.com
Montreal – Stm.info ("tous azimuts" interactive map gives customized
    directions)
Vancouver – Translink.bc.ca
Ottawa – Octranspo.com
Calgary – Calgarytransit.com (no trip planner)
Edmonton – Edmonton.ca (see online services, transit trip planner)
Quebec City – Stcuq.qc.ca (in French; no trip planner)
Hamilton – City.hamilton.on.ca/Living-Here/Transit/ (no trip planner)
Winnipeg – Winnipegtransit.com (no trip planner)
London – Londontransit.ca (interactive map gives customized directions)

Magazines

A to B Magazine – A UK-based magazine that specializes in folding bicycles,
    electric bicycles, bicycle trailers and carfree alternatives of all kinds.
    website: Atob.org.uk

Bicycling – League of American Cyclists' magazine, see their website for
    details. website: Bikeleague.org

Carbusters – Quarterly magazine critiquing car culture and exploring
    positive alternatives. Features world news, food for thought and
    action, tools for survival in car culture, interviews, cartoons and
    more. website: Carbusters.org

Telecommuting

Canadian Telework Association – A non-profit association dedicated to
    promoting telework in Canada. website: Ivc.ca/cta

June Langhoff's Telecommuting Resource Center – June calls herself a
    televangelist who promotes telecommuting and other remote work
    styles. A fun and informative website. website: Langhoff.com

The Telework Coalition – Brings together organizations, companies, and individuals with the common interest of promoting awareness and adoption of Telework and Telecommuting applications. 204 East Street, NE, Washington, DC 20002, USA; website: Telcoa.org

The Telework Consortium – Started in 2002 as a non-profit research organization focused on building the business case for telework using advanced communications and technology. 2214 Rock Hill Road, Herndon, VA 20170, USA; phone: (703) 742-7340; e-mail: telework@teleworkconsortium.org; website: Teleworkconsortium. org

Websites & Listservs

Carfree.com – From J.H. Crawford, the author of *Carfree Cities*. Publishes the online quarterly newsletter *Carfree Times*.

Carfree_cities list – A discussion forum for those interested in the carfree cities concept. Includes discussion of transport and energy issues. Companion to the presentation at Carfree.com and the newsletter *Carfree Times*. website: groups.yahoo.com/group/carfree_cities

Carfree_network list – The discussion list of World Carfree Network. Dedicated to discussing/organizing current and future projects of the network and the global carfree movement. website: Worldcarfree. net/listservs/

CarFree Yahoo Group – This list explores issues relevant to reducing or eliminating the reliance on automotive transport at a personal and societal level. website: Groups.yahoo.com/group/CarFree

Cuttingyourcaruse.co.uk – Anna Semylen's car-use reduction site. Anna runs a Cutting Your Car Use consultancy service and offers workshops on reducing car use in the UK.

Ecoplan.org – somewhat difficult to navigate, but includes lots of information about car sharing, carfree days and a range of other transportation issues.

Lesstraffic.com – from David Engwicht, author of *Reclaiming Our Cities and Towns: Better Living With Less Traffic* and *Street Reclaiming*. Quite self-promotional but offers creative and community-oriented traffic solutions.

Appendix A:
Greyhound and Amtrak Maps

Greyhound: For up-to-date route information, visit
Greyhound.com/locations/routemap.shtml

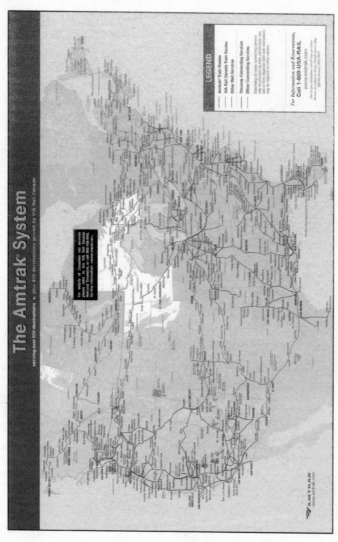

Amtrack: For up-to-date route information, visit Amtrack.com

Appendix B:
Distance, Speed & Fuel Conversion Tables

Distance
1 foot = 0.3048 meters
1 yard = 3 feet or 91.4 centimeters (nearly one meter)
1 meter = 3.279 feet (a bit over one yard)
1 kilometer = 1,090 yards or 0.6213 miles
1 mile = 1,760 yards or 1.6093 kilometers

Speed

mph	10	20	30	40	50	60	70
kph	16	32	48	64	80	96	112

Fuel Consumption
1 liter = 0.220 gallons
1 gallon = 4.546 liters
mpg = miles per gallon; mpl = miles per liter

mpg	10	15	20	25	30	35	40	45	50
mpl	2.2	3.3	4.4	5.5	6.6	7.7	8.8	9.9	11

Notes

Chapter 1: Why Cut Your Car Use?

1. "Consumer Expenditures in 2003," US Department of Labor, Bureau of Labor Statistics, June 2005, Report 986 (Bls.gov/cex/csxann 03.pdf). The 2003 mean annual household total expenditures amount to $40,817, of which $7,328 is automobile-related. As a percentage, that's 18%.
2. Ibid. (All figures in the chart are derived from the report above.)
3. "Your Driving Costs 2005," American Automobile Association, 2005 (Aaanewsroom.net/Files/Driving_Costs_2005.pdf). The figures include gasoline, oil, maintenance, tires, and depreciation, but not tolls or parking. The bicycle figures come from Bicycleuniverse.info, estimating that a bicycle owner pays $400 for a bike that lasts five years, $200 in accessories for the same time period, and $100 per year for maintenance.
4. "Summary of Travel Trends," National Household Travel Survey, US DOT, 2001: (Nhts.ornl.gov/2001/pub/STT.pdf) "Cars" includes light trucks, SUVs, etc. The 2001 survey reported that the US had more cars than drivers for the first time. To convert the per-household figures in citation 1 into per-driver figures, simply divide them by 1.8, giving $4,071 in annual automobile expenses per driver.
5. "The Real Price of Gasoline," International Center for Technology Assessment, 1998. (Icta.org/pubs/). This total includes industry tax subsidies; military expenses; and environmental, health, and social costs. (In 2004–2005, the center produced updates for costs associated with security and climate change).
6. AAA, in its 2005 "Driving Costs" booklet, estimated that on average gasoline would cost 8.5 cents per mile in 2005. When carpooling, it's easier to divide 10 cents per mile by the number of passengers. Tolls are extra.
7. "Consumer Expenditures in 2003." Amount spent on driving: $7,328. Amount spent on food: $5,340. Amount spent on apparel

and services: $1,640. Amount spent on food plus apparel and services: $6,980.

8. "In-Car Air Pollution: The Hidden Threat to Automobile Drivers," International Center for Technology Assessment, 2000. (Icta.org/pubs/)

9. Friedman, M.S., Powell, K.E., Hutwagner, L., et al. Impact of changes in transportation and commuting behaviors during the 1996 Summer Olympic games in Atlanta on air quality and childhood asthma. JAMA. 2001;285:897-905. Reviewed on PulmonaryReviews.com (Pulmonaryreviews.com/may01/pr_may01_fewer.html).

10. Makower, J. "The Green Commuter," Washington, DC, National Press Books, 1992, p. 117.

11. North Yorkshire Specialist Health Promotion Service, "Why Walk?" undated.

12. Boyd, H. et al, Health-related effects of regular cycling on a sample of previous non-exercisers: resume of main findings. Bike for Your Life Project and CTC, 1998. Findings summarized in DETR (1999), Cycling for better health, Traffic Advisory Leaflet 12/99, DETR (see Dft.gov.uk/stellent/groups/dft_roads/documents/pdf/dft_roads_pdf_5 04739.pdf)

13. UKK Institute, "Patient education and counseling," 1998, Tampere trial Finland. Reported in On Your Bike, Spring 1999.

14. Martin, Dr. S., Team leader on coronary heart disease prevention, Department of Health. Speech at Safe Routes to Schools Conference, York 30 June 1999.

15. Nationwide Personal Transportation Survey. US Department of Transportation, Federal Highway Administration, Research and Technical Support Center. Lanham, MD: Federal Highway Administration, 1997.

16. Author's calculations based on "American Time Use Survey," 2003 (Bls.gov/news.release/pdf/atus.pdf) and "Summary of Travel Trends," National Household Travel Survey, US DOT, 2001 (Nhts.ornl.gov/2001/pub/STT.pdf). The latter document states "The average US driver in 2001 drove 62.32 minutes per day." This equals 380 hours per year. It also states that the average household had 21,187 annual vehicle miles traveled (VMT) in 2001. Divide this by 1.77 drivers per household and you get a figure of 11,970 annual VMT per driver. Divide the later figure by 380 hours driven per year (see above), and we get 31.5 mph as the average speed driven. The time use survey

tells us that the average American works 6.955 hours per day (including both full- and part-time workers, over the entire year). Multiplied by 365 days, the average wage earner works 2,539 hours per year. If we take 15% of these hours (the portion of personal income spent on cars, being $5,637 of $37,382; based on per-household figures divided by 1.3 earners per household), we get 381 hours on average worked per wage earner per year to pay for his/her car(s). Your author added a conservative 64 hours per year in time spent maintaining, repairing, cleaning, searching for, parking, etc., one's car. The 380 hours actually driven plus the 381 hours spent working to pay for driving plus the 64 hours in other car time equals a total of 825 hours per year. 11,970 miles driven divided by 825 hours equals 14.5 mph as an estimated average "real speed." Even if we use AAA's figures (by which we'd have higher expenses and drive 3,000 miles more), the "real speed" comes out essentially the same.

Chapter 2: How are You Using Your Car?

1. DETR (now DfT), "Preparing Your Organisation for Transport in the Future: The Benefits of Green Transport Plans," June 1999.
2. "Daily Travel Quick Facts," US Bureau of Transportation Statistics, National Household Travel Survey, 2001–2002 (Bts.gov/programs/national_household_travel_survey/daily_travel.html)
3. TransportEnergy, "Best Practice Programme: A Travel Plan Resources Pack for Employers," 2003 and DfT "Making Travel Plans Work," July 2002.
4. (Saferoutestoschools.org/pdfs/SafetyTalkingPoints.pdf)
5. (Nhtsa.dot.gov/people/injury/buses/GTSS/case4.html)
6. "National Household Travel Survey Daily Travel Quick Facts," based on National Household Travel Survey, US DOT, 2001–2002 (Bts.gov/programs/national_household_travel_survey/daily_travel.html). The reasons for daily trips in the USA are divided as follows: 45% for shopping and errands, 27% for social and recreational purposes, and 15% for commuting.
7. "Eating Oil: Food in a Changing Climate," Sustain/Elm Farm Research Centre, December 2001. (Sustainweb.org/pdf/eatoil_sumary.pdf).

Chapter 3: Looking at the Alternatives

1. (Walking.about.com/od/healthbenefits/).
2. "Transportation and Health" fact sheet, Surface Transportation Policy Project, Washington, DC. (Transact.org/library/factsheets/health.asp).
3. "Journey to Work Trends in the United States and its Major Metropolitan Areas: 1960–2000," US Department of Transportation, Federal Highway Administration, 2003, Publication No. FHWA-EP-03-058 (Fhwa.dot.gov/ctpp/jtw/). Statistics Canada, Commuting to Work: Highlight Tables, 2001 Census (Statcan.ca).
4. Ibid.
5. "Your Driving Costs 2005," AAA, 2005. Cost of owning and operating a new domestic car, over a five-year period, when traveling 15,000 miles per year: $8,410. Divided by 365 days: $23. The taxi reference was added by your author.
6. Rodale Press Survey, quoted in H.R. 1265-Bicycle Commuter Act, (Bikeleague.org/educenter/hr1265.htm).
7. Pucher, John, (professor at the Department of Urban Planning, Rutgers University), "Let's Get Those Pedals Pumping!" (Policy.rutgers.edu/faculty/pucher.html).
8. US Department of Transportation, Federal Highway Administration, "National Bicycling and Walking Study: Transportation Choices for a Changing America," 1994, p. 2.
9. Newton E., "Cycle security," *Bicycle* magazine, 1998; 3:38–42.

Local Public Transportation
10. Snell, Bradford C., 1974, "American Ground Transport" (Worldcarfree.net/resources/free.php). See also the film "Taken for a Ride" (Newday.com/films/Taken_for_a_Ride.html).
11. American Public Transit Association fact sheets "Public Transportation: Works for America" and "Public Transportation: The Federal Partnership"
12. US Department of Transportation, Bureau of Transportation Statistics, "National Transportation Statistics 2005," (Bts.gov/publications/national_transportation_statistics/2005/html/table_02_01.html). Figures show 43,000 a year in US road fatalities and under 1,000 in US rail fatalities.

13. Smart Moves, Semlyen, A., "What are my car costs?," April 1999. British study compares fixed ownership costs of £1,640 p.a. add up your car costs calculation of a Renault Clio, a second car owned by Guy Jillings 2003, to car rental rate of £32 per day from Budget Rent-A-Car York, March 2003.

14. (Zipcar.com/carsharing-greenbenefits/).

15. "While gasoline powered motorcycles (including motorbikes, scooters, mopeds) account for a small % of vehicles in use, they are extremely polluting, producing a disproportionate amount of emissions and noise for their size. A typical motor scooter produces 3x the carbon monoxide and hydrocarbon emissions as a large diesel truck, and 8–10x as the average automobile." (Vectrixusa. com/scooter/environment.html).

Chapter 4: Changing Your Travel Habits

1. Nationwide Personal Transportation Survey. US Department of Transportation, Federal Highway Administration, Research and Technical Support Center. Lanham, MD: Federal Highway Administration, 1997.

2. US Bureau of Transportation Statistics, National Household Travel Survey, 2001–2002, Daily Travel Quick Facts, (Bts.gov/programs/ national_household_travel_survey/daily_travel.html).

Chapter 5: Making Better Use of Your Car

1. American Automobile Association, "Your Driving Costs 2005," 2005. "AAA estimates the average new car will depreciate $3,879 per year of ownership."

2. "As Rugged Vehicles Take to the Streets, Gas Prices Take Off," The New York Times, June 25, 1995, p. 1.

3. Energy Efficiency Best Practice Programme, "That's an Idea," September 1998.

4. Gordon, Deborah, "Steering a New Course," Union of Concerned Scientists, Cambridge, MA, 1991.

5. Makower, J., "The Green Commuter," National Press Books, 1992, p. 61.

6. (Fetinsurance.com/speed.htm).

7. T.R.L, Taylor, M., Lynam, D., Baruya, A., "The Effects of Driver's Speed on the Frequency of Road Accidents," TRL Report 421.

8. DfT, "Vehicle Speeds Great Britain", 2001, Statistics Bulletin (02) Table 5, urban roads. Another source: (Activelivingresources.org/first_steps.html).

9. Green, Stephen, "Effort to Up Speed Limit May Take Time," *Sacramento Bee*, October 23, 1995, p. A1.

10. Energy Efficiency Best Practice Programme, "That's an Idea," September 1998.

11. Energy Efficiency Best Practice Programme, "That's an Idea," September 1998.

12. (ConsumerReports.org).

13. *Permaculture* magazine (ad), 1999;19:2.

14. Cradle to the Grave study, Umwelt-und Prognose-Institut Heidelberg (Handschuhsheimer Landstr. 118a, 69121 Heidelberg, Germany. This study found that, with a typical German car being driven 13,000 km (8,077 miles) per year over a 10-year lifetime, driving accounted for only 40% of the car's "cradle to grave" pollution. The study claims that cars emit 56% of their pollution before they ever hit the road, and 4% after they are retired. However, figures for North America would certainly show a lower percentage of total pollution from the non-driving live-stages. According to the U.S. Department of Trans-portation, American cars are driven 12,200 miles per year on average, and the average life span of a vehicle is 12 years or 128,500 miles.

15. University of Utah ecologist Jeffrey Dukes calculated in 2003 that we would need to harvest 22% of the world's land plants just to equal the fossil fuel energy used in 1997 alone: (Globalecology.stanford.edu/DGE/Dukes/Dukes_ClimChange1.pdf).

16. Alternet interview with Lester Brown, by Terrence McNally, "What is Plan B?", February 2, 2006 (Alternet.org/story/31679/). See also Monbiot, George, "Feeding Cars, Not People," *The Guardian*, November 23, 2004 (Monbiot.com/archives/2004/11/23/feeding-cars-not-people/).

17. Brown, Lester, *Plan B 2.0*, Chapter 2, (Earth-policy.org/Books/PB2/PB2ch2_ss5.htm).

18. (Rainforestportal.org/articles/reader.asp?linkid=53250).

19. Monbiot, George, "Worse Than Fossil Fuel," *The Guardian*, December 6, 2004 (Monbiot.com/archives/2005/12/06/worse-than-fossil-fuel/).

20. "Hybrid-Car Tinkerers Scoff at No-Plug-In Rule," *New York Times*, April 2, 2005.

21. The $3,150 estimate was calculated by the American Council for an Energy Efficient Economy (ACEEE); the exact amounts of the credit per make/model are to be provided by the IRS in an official announcement. See (Hybridcars.com/tax-deductions-credits.html) or search for the latest article on www.irs.gov under the title "Clean Fuel Tax Deduction For Hybrid Vehicles." The current tax deduction will begin to be phased out once a given automaker produces 60,000 hybrid vehicles. By early 2007, the credit may no longer be available on the popular Toyota Prius, for example, but buyers will have longer for other makes and models.

22. (Greencarcongress.com/2004/12/on_the_wings_of.html).

23. See (Motoring.gov.uk/going_green), April 2003.

24. See (Doh.gov.uk/comeap.statementsreports/diesel.htm).

Chapter 6: Living Without a Car

1. Bicycle Association, "Cycle Bags: How to Carry Things on a Bicycle," 1995.

Chapter 7: Carfree Places

1. Scheurer, Jan, "Car-Free Housing in European Cities: A Survey of Sustainable Residential Development Projects," 2001 (Worldcarfree. netiresources/free.php). See also (Autofrei-wohnen.de) for a list of additional projects.

2. Gehl, Jan with Lars Gemzoe, *Public Space – Public Life*, The Danish Architectural Press, 2001. Book describes the transformation of central Copenhagen over a 40-year period.

3. (Carfreecity.us/study.html).

Chapter 8: Talking to Your Employer

1. ESRC Transport Research Unit at UCL, Adrian Davis Associates and Transport 2000, "Making Travel Plans Work", research report. DfT 2002.

Chapter 10: The Rebound Effect

1. Cairns, S., Hass-Klau, C. and Goodwin, P. "Traffic Impact of Highway Capacity Reductions: Assessment of the Evidence," Landor Publishing, London, 1998. Also, Goodwin, P., et al. "Evidence on the Effects of Road Capacity Reduction on Traffic Levels": Worldcarfree. net/resources/free.php

Acknowledgments

To Annie Jowett, for providing research and editing assistance, and for helping to decipher British terminology. To Ingrid Witvoet, Beth Anne Sobieszczyk, and Chris and Judith Plant at New Society Publishers for their help and support. To Cherie Seymore at Flexcar for putting me in touch with Barbara Scott and Toby Weymiller, who were both profiled as "success stories." To Dianne Olansky at PEDS in Atlanta for connecting me with Al Tiede, the proud father of Blake Tiede, the featured nine-year-old lobbyist. To Deborah Varnado at Amtrak and Kirk Dougherty at Greyhound for providing the maps that appear in the book. Thanks most of all to Anna Semlyen for writing the British version of this book.

About the Author

Randall Ghent is car-free by choice. At home and in his travels, he most always gets around by walking, cycling and public transportation. Originally from the San Francisco Bay Area, Randall is now co-director of World Carfree Network's international coordination center in Prague, Czech Republic (Worldcarfree.net), where he has edited two other books on the subject. He enjoys cooking, traveling, reading, gardening and outdoor sports. To learn more about this book, see CuttingYour CarUse.com.

Anna Semlyen wrote the British version of this book, on which the North American edition is based. Anna runs a Cutting Your Car Use consultancy service and offers workshops on reducing car use (see Cuttingyourcaruse.co.uk). She enjoys teaching yoga and juggling, and also campaigns for local children's spaces in York, UK.

Feedback is most welcome. Please let us know of other organizations you think should be in this directory, new addresses or about services or products that help to cut car use.

info@cuttingyourcaruse.com
Randall Ghent
c/o New Society Publishers,
P.O. Box 189, Gabriola Island, BC, V0R 1X0, Canada

If you have enjoyed *Cutting Your Car Use,* you might also enjoy other
BOOKS TO BUILD A NEW SOCIETY
Our books provide positive solutions for people who want to
make a difference. We specialize in:

Sustainable Living • Ecological Design and Planning
Natural Building & Appropriate Technology
Environment and Justice • Conscientious Commerce
Progressive Leadership • Resistance and Community • Nonviolence
Educational and Parenting Resources

New Society Publishers

ENVIRONMENTAL BENEFITS STATEMENT

New Society Publishers has chosen to produce this book on recycled paper made with 100% post consumer waste, processed chlorine free, and old growth free.

For every 5,000 books printed, New Society saves the following resources:[1]

14	Trees
1,234	Pounds of Solid Waste
1,358	Gallons of Water
1,771	Kilowatt Hours of Electricity
2,243	Pounds of Greenhouse Gases
10	Pounds of HAPs, VOCs, and AOX Combined
3	Cubic Yards of Landfill Space

[1]Environmental benefits are calculated based on research done by the Environmental Defense Fund and other members of the Paper Task Force who study the environmental impacts of the paper industry.

*For a full list of NSP's titles, please call 1-800-567-6772
or check out our web site at:*

www.newsociety.com

NEW SOCIETY PUBLISHERS